HE'S LIVING THE AMERICAN DREAM—
AND YOU CAN TOO!

Richard M. DeVos
. . . is co-founder and president of Amway, the phenomenally successful Michigan corporation. DeVos is rich—and enjoys it. He works hard—and loves it. He believes in decency and in God—and these old-fashioned, durable principles are the foundation of his rewarding life.

BELIEVE!

The inspiring, practical, up-beat philosophy that
- challenges you to recognize your limitless possibilities for achievement . . .
- helps you to aim high and go confidently after the things you want from life . . .
- encourages you to love patriotism and your God.

BELIEVE!

The book that can turn you around and set you straight—right on the path to success and fulfillment.

Believe!

by Richard M. DeVos
with Charles Paul Conn

PUBLISHED BY POCKET BOOKS NEW YORK

Scripture quotations in this volume are from the King James Version of the Bible.

"One Ship Drives East" by Ella Wheeler Wilcox is reprinted by permission of Rand McNally & Company.

Information concerning resources and production were verified in *Statistical Abstracts of the United States 1974*, 95th edition, published by the U.S. Bureau of the Census, copyright, ©, July, 1974, by the Department of Commerce.

This book is a joint effort. The introductory material to each chapter is by Charles Paul Conn. The chapter texts are by Richard M. DeVos.

POCKET BOOKS, a Simon & Schuster division of
GULF & WESTERN CORPORATION
1230 Avenue of the Americas, New York, N.Y. 10020

Copyright © 1975 by Richard M. DeVos

Published by arrangement with Fleming H. Revell Company
Library of Congress Catalog Card Number: 75-4883

ISBN: 0-671-45829-9

20   19   18   17

POCKET and colophon are trademarks of Simon & Schuster.

Printed in the U.S.A.

TO my wife Helen
and our children
Dick, Dan, Cheri, Doug
whom I love very much

Contents

CONTENTS

Preface

This book is not intended to be a story of my life, but rather a statement of some of the things I believe. If it were a story of my life, I would have had to tell you about my weaknesses and shortcomings. Therefore, I am thankful to my close personal friends for loving me even though they know me well; and I am thankful to God, who loves me despite the weaknesses, and who uses all of us in spite of ourselves. I thank Him for all that I am and have, and for helping me to realize that He can take someone like me and make all this happen.

RICHARD M. DEVOS

Foreword

Sitting on the platform, I wondered: How will I introduce Rich DeVos in one minute? Years of relationship . . . days of fellowship . . . hours of discussion, laughter, and prayer . . . in one minute? Impossible!

I jotted some notes—the typical introduction of a well-known man:

- —one of the great success stories of all times
- —a public speaker who spellbinds thousands motivating them to be and to do
- —a man who loves his wife and considers her advice and counsel important
- —a real family man who invests time with his children and spends energy on them
- —a philanthropist who gives to public causes but also supports private needs
- —a leader among leaders—sought after for his ability to think—constantly making new friends but still intimate with

those who knew him as a young dreamer.

I glanced at Rich. He was eager to speak —excited—knowing he had a message worth sharing. He is a Christian—dedicated, concerned, and active—a magnetic personality who is not ashamed of the Gospel of Christ. My notes said all this and more, yet somehow they seemed clinical. Why tell the obvious? I have known Rich all these years. Tell the audience what this man is *really* like.

I put the notes aside. I waited my turn. I approached the rostrum. Let me tell you a little of what Rich DeVos has meant to me:

—He always has time to see me or take my calls, even in the middle of important meetings, and usually when it will cost him money.

—Every material thing that Rich and Helen have they have shared with Marilyn and me and our children—private jets, yachts, sailboats, summer and winter homes—all of these—in addition they have given us their most important gift—the gift of themselves.

—Years ago, when Amway was young and our friendship new, my wife, Marilyn, called Amway for two fire extinguishers. The only person she knew at Amway was Rich, so she called him. He drove clear across town to deliver this big order personally!

—My children call him Uncle Rich, and for good reason. He has taken our older son, Steven, on an all-day, one-thousand-mile jet tour of speaking engagements and conferences, keeping Steve by his side all day. When our son David grew tired (I was occupied preaching) Rich picked him up, carried him to the hotel, and tucked him in bed. After a fun-filled day on the sailboat, the power boat, the water skis, and the trampoline, our daughter Patty has walked hand-in-hand with Uncle Rich, to the ice cream store—Patty chattering and asking questions like, "Uncle Rich, how did you get all this stuff, anyhow?" Rich patiently supplied answers as they ate their ice cream cones.

—Having lost his own father some years ago, Rich has adopted mine and cared for him with phone calls, letters, money, and vacations.

—Helen, Rich's wife, is a very special person of great depth and understand-

ing. Rich is more than aware of this—
he is grateful for it and tells her so.

—His children, Dick, Dan, Cheri, and
Doug, evidence their own individuality,
demonstrating by their actions that they
know they are greatly loved.

—At banquets he table-hops—chatting, relating, pouring coffee—making everyone feel at ease.

—I have seen him cry over people's needs
and rejoice over souls accepting Christ.

—He prays, not as the Publican prayed,
but as a grateful sinner, transformed
by the Gospel.

—His philosophy of business, his market-
ing expertise, his innate decision-mak-
ing instincts, and management ability
have helped in the accelerating world-
wide ministry of Gospel Films.

Once when I did something stupid, Rich
said, "That was really dumb, Z." Then he
picked me up and helped me. He is that special kind of friend. He is like a blood brother.
I know his strong points and his faults. He
knows mine—yet we love each other deeply.

If, during your lifetime, you ever have
one friend like Rich DeVos, you are most
fortunate. He is honest and open, loyal and

loving—able to say, "I am sorry, I am wrong"; yet equally able to forcefully drive a point and say, "Absolutely not!"

When I think of him, I think of what Paul said in Philippians 1:3: "I thank my God upon every remembrance of you." Rich is my friend—my very real friend, and I thank God for him. Not only does he believe, he lives what he believes. What Rich believes has greatly affected my life and my ministry. Ladies and gentlemen—BELIEVE! by Richard DeVos!

BILLY ZEOLI

Believe!

1

In almost any conversation with Rich De-Vos, the single phrase one is most likely to hear is the three-word expression "Jay and I."

The individual whose name so often pops up when DeVos talks is Jay Van Andel, his business partner and a man with whom De-Vos's life is inextricably intertwined. Together they built the Amway Company and together they direct its vast operation, but their relationship is much more than simply a professional one.

Both men are of Dutch ancestry, less than two years apart in age, and both were born and reared in Grand Rapids. They met while

attending Christian High School there. As
the story goes, Van Andel owned a car, and
the younger DeVos, who didn't, agreed to
pay twenty-five cents per week for a ride
back and forth to school. The two learned
that they shared many interests, particularly a mutual desire to be independent
businessmen. And so it was that, after each
had spent a couple of years in the air force,
they started out to fulfill that ambition as
partners.

The combination worked like a charm.
The two men shared the duties and status of
chief-executive officers of the corporation,
DeVos wearing the title of president while
Van Andel is listed as chairman of the
board. They share in all policy-level decisions, and it is common to hear Amway
people marvel at the way the different abil-
ities and strengths of the two men comple-
ment each other.

The admiration which DeVos has for his
partner surfaces constantly in his speeches
and in casual conversation. "I guess Jay is
one of the smartest men I know," he says.
"Back in high school he was one of those
students who could make straight As without
ever opening a book. He has a mind that
just stores and processes information like

a computer. He can look at a problem, size it up, lay out all the pros and cons, and give the facts to back up his point of view. He's really amazing."

In the lobby of their international-head-quarters building, there are bronze statues of DeVos and Van Andel, gifts to them from the association of Amway distributors. It is fitting that the two statues, while separate, together comprise a single piece of sculpture, both cut from the same material, sharing the same base, yet distinctly different from one another. In the sculpture, as in life, they are inseparably joined to one another. They wouldn't have it any other way.

BELIEVE!

. . . in Unlimited Potential

Those people whose aim is always low generally hit what they shoot at: they aim for nothing and hit it.

Life need not be lived that way. I believe that one of the most powerful forces in the world is the will of the man who believes in himself, who dares to aim high, to go confidently after the things that he wants from life.

"I can." It is a powerful sentence: I can. It is amazing how many people can use that sentence realistically. For the overwhelming majority of people, that sentence can be a true one. It works. People can do what they believe they can do. Apart from the few people in the world who are deluded in a psychotic sense, the gap between what a man thinks he can achieve and what is actually

possible to him is very, very small. But first
he must believe that he can.

Let's get one thing straight: I do not pre-
tend to be an expert on the subject of motivation. I have no more knowledge of what
motivates men than does the average person. Since Amway has grown so rapidly,
and since its success has depended on two
hundred thousand self-employed distributors, I am often asked for my notions of
motivation. "What makes some people succeed when others fail?" they want to know.
Or they ask for my "secrets" on motivation,
as if I can deliver some profound bit of
wisdom about why one man sets new sales
records while another folds up and quits. I
hate to disappoint these people, but the simple fact is that I have no gimmicks or tricks
or magic words to make people succeed.

But although I cannot claim any special
knowledge of motivational technique, I do
have a firm conviction that almost anyone
can do whatever he really believes he can
do.

The nature of the goal really makes little
difference. When I was a young man, I had
an ambition to go into business for myself
and succeed at it. That was "my thing," as
the current expression has it. I was not par-

ticularly interested in finishing college, or traveling around the world, or becoming the leading golfer on the PGA tour or the top man in the Michigan legislature. There is nothing wrong with those things—they all are legitimate goals—but they just didn't happen to appeal to me at the time. My goal was to succeed in my own business, and I believed that I could do it.

There is no way ever to know for sure, of course, but I believe the result would have been much the same whatever my goal had been. The point is that there are no areas of life which are immune to the combination of faith and effort. The personal philosophy of "I can" does not apply just to business but to politics, education, church work, athletics, the arts, you name it. It cuts across all lines. It can be the greatest common factor in such diverse accomplishments as earning a Ph. D., making a million dollars, becoming a five-star general, or riding a winner at Churchill Downs.

I look back at the forty-odd years of my life, and it seems that, more than any other single lesson, my experiences have conspired to teach me the value of determined, confident effort. For most of my life, I have been associated with Jay Van Andel. We started the Amway company together in 1959, but long before that—since we were teen-agers in high school, in fact—we were sharing experiences that taught us forcibly the excitement of "I can."

When World War II ended Jay and I came home convinced that the aviation business was the hot item of the future. We had visions of airplanes in every garage, millions of people learning to fly, that sort of thing. So we wanted to go into the aviation business. We had a few hundred dollars, bought a little Piper Cub airplane, and got ready to open an aviation school. There was a minor problem: neither of us knew how to fly an airplane!

We didn't let that stop us. We simply hired experienced pilots to give the flying lessons, while we stayed busy with the work of selling those lessons to the public. The point is that we had decided to operate a flying service, and we refused to let anything dampen our enthusiasm—not even a small detail like not knowing how to fly.

We hit another snag—when we got our customers signed up and our instructors hired, we discovered that the runways at the little airport had not been completed yet. They were still nothing but giant streaks of

mud. We improvised. A river ran alongside
the airport, so we bought some floats for our
Piper Cub and flew right off the water, taking off and landing on those bloated pon-
toon floats. (We eventually had two students who graduated from our course who
had never landed an airplane on dry land!)

We were supposed to have offices there at
the little airstrip, but the time came to open
our business and the offices were still not
built. Something had to be done. A chicken
coop was bought from a farmer down the
road, hauled over to the airstrip, white-
washed, a padlock put on the door, and a
sign hung that read grandly: WOLVERINE AIR
SERVICE. We had set out to get into the aviation business and we were in it.

The end of that story is that we built a
thriving business, bought a dozen airplanes,
and eventually had one of the biggest aviation services in town. But we made it only
because from the very start, we believed in
ourselves. We felt in our bones that we could
do it, and we did, despite those early road-
blocks. If we had launched the project half-
heartedly, not quite believing in it, always
looking over our shoulders for an excuse to
lie down and quit, the first plane would
never have made the first flight—there

never would have been a Wolverine Air Service.

That story illustrates a basic point: one never knows what he might accomplish until he tries. That is so simple that some people completely overlook it. If we had listened to all the logical arguments against our air service in those days, we would never have attempted it. We would have given up before we started, and to this day we would assume that we could not have made a go of it. We would still sit around and talk about that great idea that didn't work. But it did work, because we believed in it and committed ourselves enough to try it.

Also, after that we decided to try our hands at the restaurant business. Not that we knew anything at all about the restaurant business—we didn't—but we had been out to California and seen drive-in restaurants for the first time. Grand Rapids had nothing like that, we thought, and we believed we could make a drive-in restaurant go in our hometown. So we tried it. We bought a prefabricated building, put a one-man kitchen inside, and were all ready for the grand opening. When opening night came, the power company had not connected the electricity. Temporary panic. But

we never once entertained the idea of post-
poning the opening. We rented a generator
at the last minute, set it up in that squatty
little building, and cranked out our own
electricity. The restaurant opened right on
schedule.

That little restaurant never became the
biggest money-maker in the world, but it
was a going venture. One day Jay would
cook while I hopped cars; the next day we
would reverse roles. (It was a terrible way
to try to make a living!) But the important
thing is that we put our minds to doing the
thing we had set out to do, instead of just
sitting around and talking about it. We
could have talked about it for years. We
could have worried about all the problems
and reflected on the obstacles and never
gotten around to *doing* it. So we would never
have known whether or not we could succeed in the restaurant business.

What does all this say? Give things a
chance to happen! Give success a chance to
happen! It is impossible to win the race unless you venture to run, impossible to win
the victory unless you dare to battle. No life
is more tragic than that of the individual
who nurses a dream, an ambition, always
wishing and hoping, but never giving it a

chance to happen. He nurses the flickering dream, but never lets it break out into flame. Millions of people are that way about having a second income, or owning their own business, and Amway is designed somewhat in response to that need. There are millions more who nurture private, almost secret dreams in other areas: the schoolteacher who wants to go back for that master's degree; the small businessman who dreams of expanding his business; the couple who has intended to make that trip to Europe; the housewife whose ambition is to write short stories for the free-lance market. The list could go on and on. People dreaming but never daring, never willing to say, "I can," never trusting their dreams to the real world of action and effort—people, in short, who are so afraid of failure that they fail.

For the individual in that position, there is only one thing left after all the arguments are weighed and all the costs measured. Do it. Try it. Quit talking about it and do it. How will you ever know if you can paint that picture, run that business, sell that vacuum cleaner, earn that degree, hold that office, make that speech, win that game, marry that girl, write that book, bake that soufflé, build that house—unless you try it!

My early experiences with Jay were so dominated with this kind of attitude that we did things which, looking back, seem almost foolhardy. But we were so eager to try our hand at new things and so confident that they would come out right that we just floated along on a cloud of "I can." And usually we found that we could! But to know that, first we had to try.

We read a book—before either of us was married—that really turned us on to sailing. The book was written by a fellow who had sailed around the Caribbean, and it was filled with the adventures of the high seas. So we decided to sail to South America. We had worked hard and deserved a break, a vacation. We bought an old thirty-eight-foot schooner in Connecticut and got ready for a big trip. We planned to sail down the eastern coast of the United States to Florida and then over to Cuba, then down through the Caribbean to see all the exotic islands, and eventually wind up in South America. We were going to have a wonderful time. The only problem was that neither of us had ever been on a sailboat in our lives. Never.

I remember going to Holland, Michigan, one day and asking a fellow in a sailboat to give us a ride. "Why should I give you a ride?" he asked.

I said, "Well, we just bought a thirty-eight-footer and we've never sailed in our lives."

"Where are you planning to go in it?" he asked. And when we told him South America he almost passed out right on the dock.

But we believed we could.

We picked up our boat, got a few quick lessons, and set sail with the book in one hand and the tiller in the other. We got lost immediately. We got lost so badly in New Jersey that even the Coast Guard couldn't find us. We missed two turns at night and got way back up in the inland marshes someplace. When the Coast Guard finally found us after an all-day search, they couldn't believe where we were. "Nobody has ever been this far inland in a boat this size before," they declared, and hauled us unceremoniously back out to the ocean with a rope.

That was a wonderful old boat, except for a habit it developed of leaking, which might be considered a rather bad habit for a boat. We finally got to Florida, pumping water out of the bottom of that boat all the way. We would set the alarm for three o'clock every morning to get up and put the pump on, or by five o'clock we would practically be bailing water out by hand. By the time we got to Havana, the situation improved and we hoped our troubles were over. We turned down the northern coast of Cuba, and one dark night the old schooner just gave up and began to sink in fifteen hundred feet of water, ten miles off the coast. The first ship that came in sight was a big Dutch ship—which would have made a beautiful ending to the story, since Jay and I are both of Dutch ancestry, except this Dutch ship wouldn't pick us up. The men on board just radioed and reported that they had spotted a crummy old Cuban boat in distress and went on their way. An hour later an American ship from New Orleans picked us up and deposited us in Puerto Rico.

Did we give up then and go home?

We didn't even consider it. We had arrived in Puerto Rico in a fashion different from our plans, to be sure, but we were there nevertheless. Back home in Michigan our folks thought, "Oh well, now those two young boys will be coming home." The thought never occurred to us. We notified our insurance company, told them where to send the money, and kept right on traveling. We went all through the Caribbean, through the major countries of South America, and eventually returned to Michigan right on schedule.

That trip was not a matter of life-or-death importance; it wasn't as significant as a career or a family; it was just a trip, a lark, a time for two young guys to get out and see a little piece of the world. But it came at a meaningful time for me, because it reinforced this growing conviction that the only thing that stands between a man and what he wants from life is often merely the will to try it and the faith to believe that it is possible. After thirty years in business nothing I have learned has weakened that conviction.

Why do so many people let their dreams die unlived? The biggest reason, I suppose, is the negative, cynical attitudes of other people. Those other people are not enemies —they are friends, even family members. Our enemies never bother us greatly; we can usually handle them with little trouble. But our friends—if they are naysayers, constantly punching holes in our dreams with a cynical smile here, a put-down there, a constant stream of negative vibrations—our friends can kill us! A man gets excited about the possibility of a new job. He sees the opportunity to make more money, do more meaningful work, rise to a personal challenge; the old heart starts pounding and the juices begin to flow and he feels himself revving up for this stimulating new prospect. But then he tells his neighbor about it over the back fence one evening. He gets a smirk, a laugh that says, "You can't do that," a foot-long list of all the problems and obstacles, and fifty reasons why he never will make it and is better off to stay where he is.

Before he knows it, his enthusiasm falls down to near zero. He goes back into the house like a whipped pup with his tail dragging the ground and all the fire and self-confidence is gone and he begins to second-guess himself. Now he is thinking of all the reasons that he *can't* make it instead of the reasons that he can. He lets one five-minute spiel of negativism or ridicule or just plain disbelief from a dream-nothing, do-nothing neighbor take the the steam right out of his engine. Friends like that can do more damage than a dozen enemies.

A young housewife decides to take knitting lessons so she can knit sweaters, afghans, all sorts of things. She gets a book and the needles and yarn and starts to learn

the simplest knitting steps, full of visions
of brightly colored mittens and clothes.
Then her husband comes home from work
and tells her how hard it is to knit, how
she'll have to work years to be any good at
it, how many women have started and quit.
He gives her one of those patented, patro-
nizing smiles that says, "You'll never learn
to knit very well, you poor thing." And before he has left the room she is believing
more in his cynicism than in her faith.

Remember that the easiest thing to find
on God's green earth is someone to tell you
all the things you cannot do. Someone will
always be eager to point out to you—perhaps merely with a look or a tone of voice—
that anything new or daring which you try
is hopelessly doomed to failure. Don't listen
to them! It is always the fellow who has
never made ten thousand dollars a year who
knows all the reasons why you can't make
fifteen thousand. In the Boy Scouts, it is
always the tenderfoot who can recite the
reasons that you can't make Eagle Scout. It
is the college flunk-out who can explain why
you are too dumb to get that degree; the fellow who never ran a business who can best
describe the obstacles that make it impossible to get started; the girl who never en-

tered a golf tournament who can most convincingly tell you why you don't have a chance to win. Don't listen to them! If you have a dream, whatever it is, dare to believe it and to try it. Give it a chance to happen! Don't let your brother-in-law or your plumber or your husband's fishing buddy or the guy in the next office rob you of that faith in yourself that makes things happen. Don't let the guys who lie on the couch and watch television every night tell you how futile life is. If you have that flame of a dream down inside you somewhere, thank God for it, and do something about it. And don't let anyone else blow it out.

My father was a great believer in the potential of individual effort. Every time he heard me say the word "can't" as a boy, he would say, "There is no such word as 'can't,' and if you say it one more time I'll knock your block right through that wall!" He never did that, but I never forgot the point he was making. I learned that there really are no good uses of the word "can't."

Believe you can, and you'll find that you can! Try! You'll be surprised at how many good things can happen.

2

His name is Timothy and he is a personal aide to DeVos. His assignment is Rich De-Vos. Day and night. From the time he leaves his home each morning until he returns at night, DeVos has a shadow named Timothy. He is tall and athletic, with a country-boy-gentle face and a pleasant manner. Maybe Timothy knows DeVos better than anybody.

He is hunched over a cup of coffee now at the Howard Johnson's restaurant in Grand Rapids. The rain is cold and steady outside and he is in a talkative mood. "Yeah, I like my job. I sure do. I have to be away from home a lot, but it's worth it, and my wife, she understands."

It is not difficult to get Timothy to talk about his boss. "I tell you, DeVos is some kinda great guy. When I first got this job, I wasn't sure I could take it, you know, being with one guy that close all the time. But it's worked out fine. I may not enjoy it with someone else. I don't know. But I enjoy it like it is now.

"He travels a lot, and of course I'm right there with him. But there's another fella that spells me, so if I'm gone from home for several days, I usually get a few days off.

"My wife's about to have a baby. I don't really mind either way—boy or girl—you know? But the baby's due in about a week and so they gave me two weeks off starting day after tomorrow. They're really good about things like that."

Does DeVos ever lose his temper, ever show an unpleasant side, ever get angry or impatient?

"Never has. No, never has. He's just not the kinda guy that gets uptight with you, you know? Like when things don't go just right, or somebody doesn't do something right—he just sorta rolls with it. A really flexible guy—you know what I mean?"

Timothy takes another long drag on his cup of coffee, and adds, "It's remarkable, really. I mean, for a man as important as he is, with all that money, to be so easy to get along with. You just wouldn't believe it."

BELIEVE!

... in Accountability

The concept of accountability goes all the way back to the Garden of Eden; it is as old as man himself. Adam and Eve tasted the apple and, before the day was over, were held accountable for what they had done. After trying to finesse the issue with the fig leaves and all that, they accepted responsibility for what they had done and were driven from the garden.

Just as we can trace the concept of accountability back to Adam and Eve, we need go only to Cain and Abel to find an example of someone trying to escape accountability for his behavior. Cain killed Abel, then gave the world its first lesson in passing the buck. When Jehovah called on Cain for a reckoning for Abel's death, the murdering brother countered with a response that still stands as a classic example of the evasive nonanswer: "Am I my brother's keeper?" (Genesis 4:9)

The answer, of course, was yes. Yes, Cain was accountable. Just as Adam and Eve were accountable. Just as you and I are accountable. Accountability—the demand that each individual takes full responsibility for his choices and actions, the willingness to accept the rewards or punishment that follow as natural consequences of his behavior. Accountability is the glue that holds a society together. It is the common agreement by the members of any society that they will be responsible in their dealings with one another. Accountability is having to answer to someone for what one does.

Everyone is accountable to someone—or should be. The employees of a manufacturing company draw their per-hour wages at the end of the week, and consequently are accountable to their foreman for how they spend time on the job during that week. The foreman, on the other hand, is accountable to the supervisor, and he to the manager, and so forth, to the chief executive officer of the company for the level of productivity in his part of the plant. The president is in turn answerable to the board of directors, and the board of directors is answerable to the stockholders, who have invested their money and expect a profit in return. At each point along the ladder, the specific concerns of individuals are different, but everyone along the way must answer to someone else for his actions. Even the stockholders or owners of the company must answer to the government, and the government is in turn answerable to the people, which brings the accountability full circle.

We have always held that the man who breaks a jewelry-store window and steals a diamond is answerable to the laws of the land. If he is caught, he is held accountable, and he must take the consequences. On the other hand, the man who works hard to save a million dollars, or build a beautiful farm, or earn a college degree is regarded as having the right to enjoy the advantages which accrue to that diligence. Consequences are inextricably tied to behavior. Good behavior is automatically rewarded. Bad behavior is automatically punished. In either case, the underlying concept is that every individual is accountable to society— he is answerable for his own behavior.

As basic as such a concept is to the give-and-take of organized society, still it is being challenged in modern times. I am not sure exactly who is to blame—some say that psychology is the culprit—but there is a theory gaining support in the land that people should not be judged and held answerable for their behavior. If a kid fools around in school, never studies, and a teacher wants to flunk him, it is becoming increasingly popular to say that it isn't the kid's fault. He must have been poorly motivated, the argument goes, so he shouldn't be blamed. The fault must lie not with him but with the educational system. If a man is a chronic and habitual criminal, a ne'er-do-well who has spent most of his life bouncing in and out of jails, it is becoming fashionable to absolve him of any responsibility, blaming society for making him what he is. There must be something basically wrong with a society that would produce such a man, the argument goes, so it isn't fair to hold him accountable for what he has done. A government servant violates the public trust by lying and cheating and covering up his criminality; yet, when he is called to task, he snivels that it was the atmosphere of immorality, or the pressure from his superiors, that caused him to act illegally, and therefore he should not be held accountable.

In this particular mentality, the trick is to find the most convenient scapegoat possible to avoid taking the responsibility for one's own situation. Parents are prime targets; most of the social institutions also serve the purpose well; and, of course, if all else fails, one can always plead, "The devil made me do it!" The thread that runs through all these excuses is that they are smoke screens; they prevent the individual from looking in the mirror at the person who is really responsible for his plight.

B. F. Skinner, whose portrait adorned the cover of *Time* magazine a couple of years ago, has been called the most influential thinker of this half century. He is the psychologist who wrote the book *Beyond Freedom and Dignity*, which *The New York Times* called the most important book of the 1970s. In it Skinner spells out the manifesto of the no-accountability point of view. Man is not responsible for his behavior, Skinner says. He is constantly being manipulated by his environment and all his actions are forced on him by the conditions under which he has experienced life. No matter what he is or does, Skinner says, he could do no differently. Therefore he should not be praised for being "good" just because he engages in good behavior, nor punished for being "bad" when he behaves badly. He is never good or bad; he merely behaves according to the conditions that exist in him and around him.

I am not a behavioral scientist, and I am certainly no authority on the philosophical background of Skinner's viewpoint, but I can emphatically state that, however appealing some may find such a system from a humanistic point of view, a society built on that premise will never work. After a certain period of time, it just will not function. The work will not be done. If no one is answerable to anyone, if all behavior is equally rewarded regardless of how good or bad it is, if no individual is held accountable for his own activity, a society simply cannot continue to function.

It is doubtful that many people actively espouse such an extreme concept of no-accountability. I even doubt that many people in the United States would agree with the socialistic and communistic systems which preach that people should be rewarded according to need, regardless of their output of energy. But many people have succumbed gradually to this seductive spirit of blaming other people for their troubles, finding scapegoats for their own shortcomings, and generally refusing to take full responsibility for their own situation in life.

There are a few principles of accountability that we would do well to remember.

First, *the more one has, the greater his accountability*. That not only makes good sense, but it has scriptural support as well, in the parable of the men with different numbers of talents. Jesus told this story to speak to us about accountability (or stewardship). The man who was given five talents to invest was answerable for the full responsibility of those five talents. "To whom much is given, much is required" (*see* Luke 12:48). If we acknowledge the fact that the things which we have—health, intelligence, opportunity—come from the hand of God, then we must understand that the more we are given to work with, the more we are answerable for. A man of wealth is expected to do more in his financial contributions than a man of modest means. A person of great influence has a greater responsibility for the effect of his life on others than the anonymous guy who has little "clout" in the world. The individual born with a brilliant mind, or great talent of any kind, has a larger responsibility to use it for good than the person of limited ability.

But this principle cuts both ways, you see. It takes into account the different levels at which people start in life, and still holds that each man is answerable at the level at which he finds himself. So the man of modest income is still responsible for his use of money, however insignificant it seems to him. The person who has few friends or social contacts still must be answerable for his attitude and his influence, however limited. Helen Keller could easily have concluded that since she was blind and deaf, she was not answerable for her future. She could have insisted that she had been dealt a losing hand in life, and therefore was entitled to lie down and quit. But she didn't. She accepted full responsibility for her life, regardless of her limitations, and made it a useful and productive one. If an individual is born in the ghetto, with no money or motivation, and he finds himself discriminated against at every turn, it might be tempting for him to say, "Well, I have so many disadvantages that I am not responsible for the way my life turns out." He concludes that he has the right to lie down and quit, always blaming his condition on the circumstances of his birth. But he is still answerable for what he does with what he has.

On the whole, the Amway Corporation is made up of people who have caught the vision of taking their own responsibility for their condition in life. There are over two hundred thousand people in Amway who have decided that they want a bigger piece of the economic pie. They want more income. They want to enjoy things that they cannot afford. So instead of staying on their jobs, grumbling and complaining about inflation and that crummy old company for which they work, and decrying the terrible plight they are in, these folks have decided to do something about it. They have given up watching television every night, or that Saturday golf schedule, or that time when they formerly just sat around and did nothing, and they are out selling Amway products, and sharing the Amway program, to make extra money for the things they want but can't afford. Some of them do well at it and some don't do so well. But the point is that they have quit bellyaching about their condition and are trying to *do* something about it. I guess that is why I like them so much. They are people who have been willing to take the responsibility for themselves, regardless of their circumstances, and move forward from where they are.

A second principle of accountability is that *if one is held accountable, he must be given the freedom to make his own choices.* Accountability and freedom go hand in hand. You can't have one without the other. If I hold a manager in our plant responsible for achieving a certain level of production, I must give him the authority to reward or withhold rewards, as he sees fit, in order to get the job done. If I give my son one thousand dollars and tell him to use it for a year and make money with it, I must also give him the freedom to risk it, invest it, use it in whatever way he chooses. If I hold an individual answerable for his economic condition, I must provide a society in which he has the freedom to do a little extra, work a little harder, and be rewarded on the basis of what he produces. I must turn him loose and give him a free hand.

Communist countries pride themselves on their lack of accountability. They have avoided the vicious pressures of dog-eat-dog capitalism, they say, by providing a system in which every man's financial situation is controlled by the state, so he is not answerable to anyone for how well or how poorly he does. To make Russian citizens accountable for themselves, the Soviet government would have to give them the freedom to make money, to invest, to get ahead or fall behind, to conduct their own affairs. Without giving their people freedom of choice, it is impossible for them to be held answerable for the state of their economy.

Once again, the Scriptures teach this principle. God holds every man accountable for his moral behavior, but He also gives to every man a free will. The individual can choose to serve God or not to serve God, to blaspheme or worship, to conduct his affairs in love or in deceit—he is, in short, free to "do his own thing." God guarantees that freedom. He never forces anyone to walk the straight and narrow. But, having that freedom, every individual must then take the responsibility for his behavior, and be directly answerable to God for it.

Similarly, this country and its economic system offers the greatest possible freedom to its citizens. We have free choices in every area of life. The government does not tell a man where to work in America, as it does in many other nations. A man can walk right off one job today and into a different one tomorrow. He doesn't need permission from anyone. He is free to invest money, buy and sell goods and commodities, trade and deal on the open market, offer his services to whoever will buy—he is free to pursue whatever course seems best to him. In this country a man is free to achieve the amount and type of education he wishes. The American government does not tell this person to go to school and this one to work in a factory. He is free to travel as he pleases, to live where he pleases, to embrace whatever religion he pleases. But there accompanies all that freedom the responsibility for every American citizen to take the credit or the blame for whatever he is. With freedom goes accountability. You can't have one without the other.

A third principle to remember is that *accountability must always include evaluation*. In fact, accountability and evaluation are in a certain sense synonymous. If one is to be held responsible for his level of competence, or the quality of work he does, then it is necessary that his performance be evaluated.

One of the first danger signals that indicates this country is sliding toward no-accountability is the cry that goes up in many quarters against evaluation of individual performance. This viewpoint is most apparent in the educational system, where more and more teachers and academic theorists urge the adoption of no-grade policies. Don't give grades, they argue, because the kid who does poorly will be embarrassed and intimidated by a bad mark. Increasingly the classroom is becoming a place where grades are discarded for fear of hurting those who are at the bottom of the totem pole. Unfortunately, it is impossible to recognize and reward excellence without implicitly identifying inferior performance. But if we refuse to recognize the strong for fear of identifying the weak, we will experience a gradual decline in performance across the board. We destroy the incentive for pursuing excellence. We become oriented toward failure, not success. We spend all our time working with the people at the lower end of the scale, and never develop in children the taste for excellence that is so important to individual fulfillment.

I feel as strongly about the unnecessary intimidation of the weaker student as anyone does. I don't like to see anyone shamed or embarrassed. But if a teacher—or a plant supervisor or a coach or whoever—is forbidden to judge the weak, he has no way to reward the strong, and it is impossible to make anyone accountable for his own work.

Many educators propose grade-free systems because they are themselves reluctant to be evaluated. Try to get a schoolteacher to submit voluntarily to any straight-forward system of evaluation by students, peers, or administrators, and you will usually receive a flurry of evasive, hedging replies. Teachers want to make evaluation of their own performance so ambiguous and so inaccessible that it is meaningless. ("Only after twenty years can a teacher's success with a student be analyzed," one educator claims.) The idea is to get away from a system in which he can be directly and routinely judged and held accountable for the quality of his work. In any system of that type, the inferior worker coasts and the superior one loses his incentive.

Certainly schoolteachers are not the only group gravitating toward this nonevaluating posture. The viewpoint appears, thinly disguised, in many other places. Job security, if it means that a man cannot be fired no matter how poorly he performs, can be just another way of avoiding accountability. Automatic, across-the-board pay increases often provide for workers to be rewarded equally, regardless of their competence, and thus nullify the usefulness of meaningful evaluation. Even quota systems for the employing of ethnic and minority groups can become dodges by which direct evaluation of performance is made meaningless. As this trend continues, it becomes doubly important that we maintain a system of rewards and punishments based on direct evaluation in our schools. It is in the schools that children learn about life; and life, like it or not, is a harsh regimen in which rewards are contingent on behavior. It is a rule of life: one reaps what he sows. One accepts the consequences of his behavior. That is not an artifact of capitalism; it is a rule of nature itself. Accountability is woven into the fabric of life, and the sooner our children learn the reality of cause and effect, of reward and punishment, of accepting the natural and inevitable outcomes of one's actions, the better off they are.

We are not doing a child a favor by shielding him from the concept of accountability. When he leaves that cozy classroom, where Teacher gave him equal rewards whether he performed well or poorly, where the industrious and the goof-off were evenly praised and scolded, where there was no advantage attached to excellence and no penalty for incompetence—when Junior leaves that classroom to encounter the unblinking, un-yielding laws of life, he will be unprepared to answer for himself.

That is no favor to Junior. And that is no favor to the society he lives in. He must be-lieve, as must we all, in accountability, be-cause in the push-and-shove of life we can never escape our responsibility to one an-other. And in the end we cannot escape our responsibility to God.

3

The Amway Corporation is having a sales rally, and Rich DeVos is the speaker. The city is Minneapolis; the site for the rally is the City Auditorium. Strange. A sales rally in a civic auditorium? It would seem more appropriate in a hotel ballroom, or a meeting room. The City Auditorium? For an Amway sales rally?

But the time comes, and the place swarms with people. And with excitement. They come in all types and shapes and sorts of dress, from all over Minnesota and the surrounding area. They bring their friends. They call out to one another as they spot familiar faces. It is a Fourth-of-July picnic, a party, a celebration, a Saturday-night sing at a country church. It is a small slice of America: long hair and short hair and in-between hair; business suits and blue jeans and dresses tailored, homesewn, and off-the-rack. Most of all it is people—three thousand of them, happy and excited and not a grim face among them. They like being here. They are looking forward to something. It must be DeVos. DeVos? Giving a sales pitch? And they're looking forward to it?

Finally, after a film and some short speeches: "Ladies and gentlemen, the man whom you all came to hear . . . Rich DeVos!" Pandemonium. Standing ovation. And it is now clear that it *was* DeVos they were waiting for. He does not disappoint them. He likes them and they can tell. He is charged up by being there, stimulated by their enthusiasm. No podium. No notes. No formalities. Just a microphone and he is off and running. They relish every word, and he is enjoying it too, and you, even though you came just to watch, are caught up in the mood, too. He tells a few jokes, gives a little advice, lays down a driving fifteen minutes of grab-it-and-go, recognizes some outstanding Amway distributors, and before you know it the two hours are gone and he is closing. You realize that the hard sell never came. The sales pitch was in there somewhere, but you hardly even noticed. There was no pressure, no push, just lay-it-out-there-and-leave-it, and at 10:00 P.M. the rally is over.

DeVos shakes hands in front of the stage, is whisked to a waiting car, and in a few minutes is racing through the gates of the airport. A private Amway jet waits. He runs up the stairs, says hello to the cockpit crew, and soon is high over Lake Michigan heading for Grand Rapids. By 1:00 A.M. he will be in the hangar; by 2:00 A.M. he will be in bed; and by 9:00 A.M. he will be back at his desk, ready for another day in the life of Rich DeVos.

BELIEVE!

... in an Upward Look

Have you ever noticed how frequently things turn out badly when you expect them to? It seems to me that when I expect something bad to happen, I am never disappointed. If I wait long enough, eventually things will turn out as badly as I had feared.

But I have also noticed that the same principle works in reverse: if I expect good things to happen, they usually do! All I have to do is wait long enough, and expect good things to happen strongly enough, and it's not long before it all turns out the way I had hoped.

Life is that way. It tends to respond to our outlook, to shape itself to meet our expectations. Any psychologist will tell you that if a boy is called "thief" often enough, eventually he will steal something; if a student is constantly called "stupid," he will soon begin to behave stupidly; if an occasion is dreaded passionately enough, it certainly will prove to be as bad as its anticipation. The events of life, in their endless flux and flow, seem somehow to shake out pretty much as we expect them to. There is enough good and bad in everyone's life, enough sorrow and happiness, enough joy and pain, that any one of us can find ample excuse to look up or look down, to laugh or to cry, to see the world as a blessing or a curse.

I believe in an upward look! Given the option to read life however I choose, I believe in underlining the positive passages with a bright red pencil and skipping over the negative ones with barely a glance. I am an optimist. I know that sorrow exists, that life is not an unbroken delight; but I have been alive for over forty years, and on the balance I find the good in life more impressive than the bad. In the words of the old song, I have chosen to "accentuate the positive" and "eliminate the negative."

Charles Simmons, one of those powerful pulpit ministers of the early nineteenth century, said it this way:

Give me a positive character, with a positive faith, positive opinions and positive actions . . . rather than a negative character, with a doubting faith, wavering opinions, undecided actions and faintness of heart!

For a person who wants to be happy and productive, an upward look is not just a luxury. It is absolutely imperative. Why? Because the way one looks at life determines how he feels, how he performs, how well he gets along with other people. Negative thoughts and attitudes feed on themselves. They pile up higher and higher until the world actually becomes the grim place that they describe.

One time I drove my car into a service station to get some gasoline. It was a beautiful day and I was feeling fine. As I walked into the station, a young chap standing there said, rather unexpectedly, "How do you feel?"

I said, "I feel wonderful."

"You look sick," he said. Get the picture: this fellow wasn't a medical doctor; he wasn't an internist; he wasn't a male nurse.

I answered him, maybe a little less confidently this time, "No, I feel fine. I never felt better."

He said, "Well, you don't look so good. Your color is bad. You look yellow."

Well, I left that gas station and before I had driven a block I stopped the car and looked in the mirror to see how I felt! After I got home I kept checking for pale color, yellow jaundice, something, anything! I thought, maybe I don't feel all right after all. Maybe I have a bad liver. Maybe I'm sick and just don't know it.

The next time I went to that gas station I figured out what the problem was: they had just painted the station a sick-looking yellow, and everybody who went into the place developed a ghastly yellow look!

The point is that I had let one comment from one total stranger change my whole attitude for the rest of that day. He told me I looked sick, and before I knew it I was actually *feeling* sick! It is amazing how powerful a single negative thought can be.

On the other hand, almost any woman whom I have ever asked will admit that she has a dress or two hanging in her closet that she has worn only once, and never reached for again. And the reason that the dress was never worn a second or third time was that on the one occasion that she wore it not a person complimented it. No one noticed. Nobody walked up and said, "Oh, Janet, what a beautiful dress!" She didn't need the whole crowd to stand up and cheer, but if only one or two people had said, "My, that looks nice on you," she would have practically worn that thing out, instead of letting it hang there and gather dust.

Few things in the world are more powerful than a positive push. A smile. A word of optimism and hope. A "You can do it" when things are tough. That upward look that refuses to dwell on the negative, but keeps pointing to things that are positive and strong.

America has traditionally been a nation of an upward look. We in this country have always been eager to see the world as a positive, hopeful place, and to see ourselves and our fellow citizens as favorably as the facts would allow. I am afraid that in the last few years we may have been losing that positive, optimistic approach. We seem to be entering an era when the critic, the naysayer, the prophet of despair has become the hero of the day.

I noticed not long ago that one nationally

famous critic spoke on a large college campus and delivered his usual speech on what was wrong with everybody and everything, and the students stood up and cheered him. He became a hero merely by ripping up the leaders and institutions and traditions of the day.

We spend too much of our time looking down, finding fault, picking to pieces our systems and institutions, our colleges and churches, and—worst of all—each other. If we spend all our time finding fault, we will not have the human energy or the courage or the strength to try to solve the problems that genuinely afflict our institutions and organizations. The student who spends all his time finding fault with his college usually never gets around to helping it become a better college. If a man has a good friend, and all he does is tell that friend his faults, he will not be able to build the person up constructively or make him a better person.

In either case, the individual becomes a full-time critic and faultfinder. He becomes so obsessed with shouting about the problem that he never attempts to solve it. Finding problems is not difficult—problems are everywhere. To glorify the critic while ignoring the much greater contribution of the man who copes with and solves the problem is a monstrous injustice.

In New York City a new stage play opens on Broadway. People have worked and sweated blood over that play for months or even years. Investors were sought, scripts were written, music was composed, the theater was rented, actors and actresses learned their lines and rehearsed for weeks. Finally the play opens. Scores of people pour themselves into it—stagehands, directors, makeup crew, musicians, ushers, and curtain boys—all working hard to create something special for their audience.

But out there in the crowd somewhere sit four or five critics, and if they don't like the play, it is usually finished. It's done. On opening night the actors sit around in some crummy little joint off Broadway and wait for the morning papers to come out, and they read what a good job or what a terrible job they did, and they know that on the basis of that criticism from four or five people the show will fold in a matter of weeks, or go on to a long run.

There is nothing wrong with that so long as society doesn't make a hero out of the critic. The critic has his place. He has a legitimate function, and he has a job to do.

But when we reach the place where we praise the critic more for his "rip job" than we do the playwright who wrote the play, then the premium is being placed on the wrong job. It is much easier to criticize than to create. Much easier to point out the flaw in a product than to produce the goods. Much easier to tear something down than to build it. When we worship the critic, we eventually develop a nation of critics, all of them unwilling to put it all on the line and attempt to create. Rather than expose themselves to the jeers of the cynics, they do nothing at all.

Don't get me wrong. I think critics are necessary as long as we keep their role in perspective. It is a disaster to continue to focus not on men who do things, but on men who find fault with those who do things. We discredit the people who are problem solvers and praise those who point out the problem. That is the surest way I know to develop a nation of professional bellyachers! That approach produces a generation of young people who sit around discussing the deplorable shape of the world, shooting down anyone who is out there trying to do something about it.

Ralph Nader has never built a car. He

has only a limited idea of the complexity of
mass-producing a modern automobile at a
price that ten million Americans every year
can afford to pay. It doesn't take too much
savvy to find fault with your car—or your
house, your husband, or your wife. Anybody can do that. What really impresses me
is not the problems that cars have, but the
nearly miraculous accomplishment that
every finished automobile represents when
it rolls off the assembly line. I marvel at the
people who work in those factories with all
that racket and noise. I marvel at the way
they get all those pieces made in plants all
over the country and put them together.
Somebody in Timbuktu makes the grill, and
somebody else makes the emblem, somebody
else makes the seat covers, and someone else
gets all the stereo jacks to go in the right
place. Somebody puts the wiring harnesses
together and someone else gets the strip of
metal just right on the steering wheel and
tests the shock absorbers to make sure the
ride is smooth. From plants and little shops
all over the country somebody organizes all
that and gets it together so that cars come
sliding off that line like a cordwood, each
one capable of going a hundred miles an
hour with a self-contained heating-and-cool-

ing system, dozens of built-in safety devices, and a ride more comfortable than folks dreamed of a few years back.

And it all comes together like clockwork, because most of the time most of the people are doing one heck of a good job. The stereo system hooks up to the rear speaker just right and the seats match the paint job; the chrome is straight and the right tires are on the right models. Thousands of pieces come together and—wonder of wonder—the whole thing works!

To me the man who keeps all that going is the real hero. The guy who figured out how to get a steel belt inside a fiber-glass tire is a hero. That ingenious fellow who designed a muffler that lasts twice as long as the old one is a hero. Ralph Nader is a fine fellow, I'm sure. He has a part to play in our society. He is a watchdog, a professional critic, an important person to have around. But is he the hero of our little scenario? Not in my book, he's not! The real heroes are the men who have been providing America with goods and services for seventy years—the executives, scientists, designers, and workmen and housewives who make something good and positive. Without them there is nothing at all.

I don't dislike Ralph Nader. I just get tired of his constantly talking things down, constantly finding fault. And I am concerned that the attention and space in the media given to such men is creating a national climate of criticism and cynicism that will ultimately discourage the creative and the optimistic.

If the "downward look" were confined to a few nationally known critics, that would not be so bad. But sometimes ordinary people carry around with them such a negative attitude that, like the sick-yellow service station, their jaundiced view of life affects everyone around them. Just listen to the conversation today on the job, or in the coffee shop, or on the bus going to work. There is always someone who wants to talk about how things are. First it is the economy. Then it is the crime problem. Then the fact that kids are less respectful than they ought to be, or that there are too many reruns on TV, or that prices are rising too fast for a man to keep up. A man named Thomas Shepherd calls this kind of person a member of the "disaster lobby." They constantly look back to the "good ol' days" and moan for them to return. But was life really better in those days? One hundred and fifty years ago,

Shepherd points out, the average life expectancy was 38 years, the work week was 72 hours, the average pay was $275 per year. Housewives worked 98 hours a week, and there were no dishwashers or vacuum cleaners. The average person never in his lifetime heard the sound of an orchestra or traveled more than two hundred miles from his birthplace. Those were *good* ol' days? We may as well admit it—things are getting better. We are better off in most ways than any generation before us and things are bound to keep on improving.

I recently had some high-school kids on my boat, sailing on Lake Michigan. It happened that at the same time we had a crew of astronauts on the moon. One of these high-school boys said to me, "Well, that's a waste of money up there. We should have spent that money here on earth, where things are in such bad shape."

I answered him, "It was four hundred forty-five million dollars we spent on that project of putting men on the moon. What do you think we should have done with it?"

His answer came right back: "I think we should work on the poverty problem."

"Fine," I said. "How would you solve it?"

That stopped him for a minute. He replied slowly, "Well, I don't know."

I said, "Tell me how much money you need to solve the poverty problem and how you'll spend it and I'll get it for you." He asked me where I was going to get the money. "You give me a solution," I told him, "and I'll get you the money, I promise." That started a pretty lively discussion, because finally that boy was forced to quit talking in vague, general complaints and look specifically at the thing he was calling the "poverty problem." He began to think about solutions instead of merely dwelling on the problems. He put himself in the place of the fixer rather than constantly serving as the critic. And when he did that, we spent the rest of the day in a healthy, constructive discussion of the issues about which he was concerned.

It is easy never to get that far, never to get the level of one's sight off the ground and up into the sky. The richness of life, the love and joy and exhilaration of life can be found only with an upward look.

This is an exciting world. It is cram-packed with opportunity. Great moments wait around every corner. It is a world that deserves an upward look. We have heard enough from the critics and the naysayers, the cynics whose vocabularies have not progressed beyond the word *no*, the rip artists whose talent for seeing sore spots has made instant experts and heroes of them. I believe in life with a large YES and a small no. I believe that life is good, that people are good, that God is good. And I believe in affirming every day that I live, proudly and enthusiastically, that life in America under God is a positive experience!

4

The Amway story is the stuff that dreams are made of. It is a classic example of the American success story, a true-to-life case of a million-dollar company's mushrooming out of nowhere literally overnight.

It sounds like a Hollywood script, but it is nevertheless true: the Amway Corporation was born in Rich DeVos's and Jay Van Andel's basement! The year was 1959, and DeVos and Van Andel had been in business together for thirteen years. They had developed a successful distributorship for Nutrilite Products, Inc., a California-based company. By 1959 they were ready to start their own company; and, with their wives, the two men sat around a table and organized Amway.

The rest of the story is a tale of phenomenal and explosive growth. The new company operated from their basements for a while, then from a converted gas station, and finally from a small factory on a two-acre lot. Fifteen years later, the Amway plant covers over one million square feet on a three hundred-acre industrial spread. Scores of products are manufactured in a fully automated plant and shipped by a fleet of fifty tractor-trailer rigs to huge warehouses located across the country. Bottles, labels, cardboard boxes, virtually everything necessary for the Amway retail operation is manufactured on the premises. A giant computer center keeps the whole operation running smoothly. The plant's fifteen hundred employees include production workers, teams of research chemists, corporate attorneys, and data analysts. Inside the plant are new-product and quality-control laboratories, a printing plant and photo studio, and testing facilities of every description.

At the cutting edge of the company's growth is the sales force, over two hundred thousand independent Amway distributorships. Together they generate over two hundred thirty million dollars annually in estimated retail sales. In the company's history, there has never been a year when the sales graph did not climb upward. DeVos and Van Andel communicate with the distributors constantly in an endless round of sales rallies, conventions, and seminars around the country. The company offices occupy impressive quarters in the gleaming new Center of Free Enterprise, which itself attracted twenty-four thousand visitors in its first year. The company's executives crisscross the country—and travel to Amway's international operations in Canada, United Kingdom, West Germany, Australia, and Hong Kong—in a variety of vehicles that include two jet airplanes (with a full-time aviation crew of eight pilots and mechanics), buses, and a 116-foot yacht named, appropriately, the *Enterprise*.

The Amway Corporation is what free enterprise and the American dream are all about.

BELIEVE!

. . . in Free Enterprise

If you asked me what important blessing Americans most take for granted, I would have a surprising answer for you. It's not the air we breathe, or the churches we attend, or the sun that comes up every morning. Not the love of family and neighbors. Not our health or political freedom. The most grandly ignored blessing of American life is our system of free enterprise.

"Capitalism" has become virtually a dirty word in this generation, and that's a dirty shame!

Unfortunately, words like "free enterprise," "profit," and "capitalism" conjure up visions of money-hungry industrialists greedily stuffing dollars into their pockets while the poor masses become more and more destitute. Free enterprise is fast bccoming the all-purpose scapegoat of this half century. The critics will tell you that all the evils of the 1970s are laid at its door. The air and streams are polluted because of capitalism, people are poor because of capitalism, wars are fought because of capitalism. The free-enterprise system is evil, their argument goes, and it poisons the whole society.

What ignorance! What foolish, unfortunate ignorance! The truth of the matter is that the free-enterprise system is the greatest single source of our country's economic success, and its best hope for surviving the demands of this chaotic century. It is time for this generation of Americans to believe once again in free enterprise, to espouse it, to teach it to our young as a positive blessing.

Too many people consider a country's economic system irrelevant to its politics, religious life, and other cultural characteristics. That is a dangerous error. The economic system of a nation is the backdrop against which all else unfolds; it sets the stage for the entire life of a country. Many Americans ignore the blessings of free enterprise because they consider the whole issue irrelevant—a matter for the economists and the political scientists to quibble over. They wear color-coordinated clothes to air-conditioned, carpeted offices and plants, drive luxury automobiles down superhighways to spacious homes set on landscaped lawns, sit down to steak dinners before retiring to king-size beds—and hardly give a thought to the system that makes it all possible. They listen to the news on four channels, worship at whatever church they choose, give to their favorite charities, and wonder if maybe socialism *is* a better way, after all. They hear an ill-informed politican with an ax to grind berate the evils of that monstrous, dog-eat-dog capitalistic system, and wonder if maybe he might be right.

I want to challenge you to believe in free enterprise—because it *does* matter that you believe in it, understand it, and know what it is and is not.

Very simply put, free enterprise happens when the freedom of people is recognized as an inherent right stemming from the Creator, and that freedom is safeguarded (as ours is) in the structure of the government organization. In the free enterprise system, the manufacturer or businessman owns his own tools, risks his own money, sets his own prices, makes his own decisions, and makes or loses money depending on how well he provides the public with a product or service which it wants at a price it is willing to pay. Unless that company does something criminal, or violates the public interest, the government should leave him alone to pursue his interests.

The only real alternative to free enterprise is socialism or, in the extreme, communism. Under these systems the government owns the tools and factories, sets the prices, employs the workers, and provides the public with the product at a price which the government sets.

But between free enterprise and outright socialism is the condition toward which the United States is now gravitating—that of a constantly increasing governmental interference in business, where government sets more and more regulations, makes more and more decisions, owns more and more of the businesses, and slowly squeezes the corporation out of the picture.

The crucial way that an economic system must be judged is by its productive output. What does it provide for the people? What level of life does it make possible for them? Compared on that basis, free enterprise is clearly superior to alternative economic systems. Over the last two hundred years this country has outproduced any other country in the world, hands down. It has provided for its people more material goods than any other system in history.

Consider these figures from *The New York Times:* in the United States a medium-sized automobile costs about 100 days wages; in Moscow it costs about 1,000 days wages. In the United States a small refrigerator costs about 32 hours of work; in Moscow it costs about 343 hours. An average washing machine costs 53 hours here against 204 hours in the Soviet Union. Color television sets cost the equivalent of 147 hours for the American worker; in Moscow the price is 1,110 hours. The comparisons go on and on, and always the result is the same: the American system gives its workers a far greater reward for their work than does socialism or communism, its most prominent economic alternatives. And that is the ultimate test of an economic system: the degree to which it yields returns to the individual on his labor, whether that labor is by the sweat of his brow or by his managerial or creative skills.

The United States has only 6 percent of the world's population and we have about 7 percent of the land surface of the world. But, despite the fact that we are so small in comparison to the rest of the world, we as American citizens own 45 percent of all the automobiles, 60 percent of all the telephones, 30 percent of all the radios, and 80 percent of the television sets! On the production side, this country produces 25 percent of all the steel, 40 percent of the electric power, 50 percent of the corn, 60 percent of the natural gas, 30 percent of the beef, and 40 percent of all the aluminum in the world! And all of that by 6 percent of the world's population!

Of course, any time someone begins to quote statistics like that which show the overwhelming superiority of the American free-enterprise system, the critics start hollering about something they call the "quality of life." The "quality of life" is somehow lower under capitalism, they insist, even in the face of all these material goods. But I have found that it is difficult for people to worry about the quality of life when they are hungry. There is no concern for good books, good music, symphony orchestras, or a provocative intellectual climate when a man must work eighty hours a week to keep warm and fed and under a roof at

night. When a man spends all day strug-
gling to sustain himself, he has no time to
worry about the "quality of life."

The truth is that in America more people
can read, write, and speak the language than
anywhere else in the world. More people go
to church. More people receive a college
education. More people have more time and
more money for the enrichment of their
lives beyond the workaday demands of
scratching out a living. The advanced medical research of this country, the enormous
recreational programs for young people, the
hospitals and churches, the schools and
museums, the organizations that send millions of dollars overseas every month—all
these are possible only because under a free-
enterprise system there is enough material
wealth *left over* from survival needs to do
all these things. There is no United Fund in
Russia because nobody has anything to give
but the government!

Still the system is criticized. Another
popular blast leveled at free enterprise is
that under such a system there are too
many wealthy people, too many who have
too much. Once, when I was speaking on
free enterprise at a college, a young man
challenged me about the Cadillac I was

driving at the time. "If you're really concerned about the poor," he said, "why don't you give up that Cadillac you're driving and drive an old car, one that will just get you where you want to go?" What that student inaccurately believed was that if the rich have less the poor will have more. That is not the case. If those who have material wealth have less, then everyone has less. If you want the caboose to catch up with the locomotive, you don't do it by stopping the train. If the rich become poor, everyone has less.

I explained to the young man that I provided work for lots of men by buying that Cadillac. For me to be poor would not make any one of them richer. If the farmer gets less for his produce, the food doesn't get cheaper; it gets more expensive, because the farmer, having no incentive, produces less food. If America were poorer, the poorest country in Africa would be no better off. We all would have less. The only way for there to be more material wealth in the purse of the have-nots is for there to be more goods produced, and the only way to produce more is to provide incentives for people to work harder and more efficiently. And any time those incentives are provided, there will be some people who have more than others, because some will always work a little harder, do a little more to get more for themselves.

Certainly it is the responsibility of a nation to see that the rich do not take advantage of the poor, or abuse the poor, but to suggest that if the rich had less the poor would have more is a fallacy. There simply would *be* less. Those who hail socialism as a great system because in it all men are equal are right up to a certain degree. Under socialism all men are equal—they are equally poor! That is the record of history. It is clear and irrefutable.

What accounts for the massive superiority of American production over that of other systems? It is not the presence of natural resources; for, rich as our country is in natural wealth, it is easily matched and even surpassed by others. It is not that American people are smarter, or stronger, or more industrious, though that would be a pleasant vanity to entertain if it were true. It is not that we have been at it longer, because our two hundred-year history makes us practically a johnny-come-lately on the world scene. What, then, is the secret of our phenomenal productive power?

It is the system.

We have a system which allows the people to own privately the tools of production, and one which allows the man who produces more to get ahead of the man who produces less. The matter of incentive for greater productivity will come up again later. For now, let's look at the importance of private ownership of the tools.

It is the tools, after all, that make the difference. A tool may be a hammer or a steam shovel or a tractor-trailer truck or a computer or a conveyor belt. It is an instrument which a man uses that enables him to produce more with his output of energy. All over the world, men are roughly equal in energy, intelligence, and willingness to work. Italians, Indians, Czechs, Russians, Argentines, all are pretty much the same in their raw energy and ability. But a man with a tool can do more than a man without a tool. A man can work hard for eight hours digging a hole in the ground with his bare hands. A man with a pick, in the same amount of time, can dig a much bigger hole without working any harder. And a man with a bulldozer can dig a far bigger hole yet. That doesn't mean that he is a better man, or that he has any greater human value—it just means that he has a better tool.

The farmer in Spain who walks behind one old mule with a little plow and plows one acre a day is no less a person than the farmer in Kansas who plows a thousand acres a week sitting in a high-powered tractor. Once I was in Peru and saw men walking around with lumber on their backs. They carried that stuff on their backs, all bent over, from one place to another. They can move perhaps one hundred pounds ten miles in a day. One of our truck drivers climbs into the cab of a tractor-trailer rig, adjusts his cushion, slips an eight-track tape into the dash, and rolls down the highway at fifty-five miles an hour hauling thousands of pounds, day and night, without stopping. Is that truck driver a better man? No, but he has a better tool, so he produces more and lives better as a result.

It is only when one sees some of the modern tools that he can fully appreciate how powerfully a tool can change a man's ability to produce. Modern technology can put tools into a man's hands that enable him to outproduce hundreds of men without those tools. And a whole society of men with such powerful tools reaps the benefit of a work force comparable to billions of workers without tools. At our plant in Ada, Michigan, for example, we produce aerosol cans. I used to test the cans by hand, one at a time. Now we have an assembly line that produces them and cranks them out at the rate of three cans *per second!* Those cans come off the line in a blur—powerfully impressive tool! We have a computer there at Amway, and they tell me that it can print out information at the rate of eleven hundred lines per minute—that's the equivalent of one secretary typing over twenty-seven thousand words per minute, or a book-length novel in three minutes!

The list of examples is endless. It takes no time at all to recognize that it is the tools that man has which have brought him from the more primitive forms of life to the relatively rich culture of today. And the economic system which optimizes the development and use of tools will be the most productive system.

And that is exactly the point at which free enterprise has any socialistic system hopelessly beaten.

The American Economic Foundation came up with a formula that explains just how tools are the pivotal element of an economy.

The formula has been around for years, and I enjoy repeating and explaining it when I speak on free enterprise. It goes this way: $MMW = NR + HE \times T$ — Man's material welfare equals natural resources plus human energy multiplied by *tools*. All that man has of a material nature comes from the earth in some form (natural resources), but it must be converted into usable form by his own effort (human energy), whether it is physical work or mental work or whatever.

All countries have natural resources. All countries have human energy. But all countries do not have an equivalent share of material wealth. The main reason is that in some systems the people are allowed to own the tools, and in those systems the tools are better cared for and more efficiently used. In addition, those same systems give people extra benefits for developing new tools, so more new tools are developed.

People take better care of things that belong to them. That is human nature. If you don't believe it, just rent your house to someone for a year and see how well he takes care of it—or vice versa. If I don't own something, it just seems less important that I take care of it.

One day I was with some guys coming out of Los Angeles on a crowded freeway early in the morning. The smog was bad; the freeway was crowded. We got frustrated waiting to get into a line of traffic, and finally I said, "Aw, cut on in, John, it's a rented car anyway!" Suddenly it occurred to me that I would never have been so casual about banging up my own automobile. If you don't own it, you don't take care of it as well. And that is exactly the problem they have in Russia. The state owns all the tools, the factories, the buildings, the means of production, and nobody takes care of them. A psychologist, Albert Bandura, once said, "No single snowflake in an avalanche ever feels responsible." That is how it is with a sense of responsibility for tools owned by the state. It belongs to everybody, so nobody feels responsible. The tools of production—the key to material wealth—are abused and neglected and get only half the life and efficiency of privately owned tools in America.

The other aspect of the tool factor in comparing the two systems is that, in a free-enterprise system, the development of new tools is rewarded. Suppose you spent months and years working in your basement at night to invent a better plow, or a more efficient vacuum cleaner, or a sharper pair of scissors. How would you react if, when you finished that new tool, the government took it from you and said, "Thanks a lot, but this new invention now belongs to the people," and took it from you without paying you for your years of hard work and ingenuity? You would be angry, of course. You would be disillusioned and bitter and would be determined never to waste your time again developing a new tool. You worked hard while others were sleeping, watching TV, having a good time, and you got nothing for it. And so it is that in a socialistic system the incentive to develop and own new tools is squashed, and tools are developed with less frequency than in a free-enterprise system.

In America if you invented that new machine it would be yours. You would be free to sell it to the highest bidder. Or you could manufacture it and sell it by the millions. In either case, the patent law would protect your right to reap the benefit from your work. You would make money, thereby sharing the payoff of that better tool which increased someone's productive efficiency. And so you, and others like you, would be willing to do a little extra, work a little harder, explore your new ideas and convert them into reality, and as a result the whole society becomes more and more productive, and everyone lives a little better, especially those who have the initiative to go that extra step.

Free enterprise is really that simple. It is a system in which the individual has a right to conduct his business in whatever way he chooses, and keep the benefits of his work. That system is threatened whenever government burdens the businessman with rules and regulations, tells him how to operate his business, and generally increases his cost of producing goods. In the United States today the freedom of businesses to pursue their affairs is being severely limited by a flood of nit-picking, unnecessary regulations. That becomes a real danger, because as government gets more and more involved in the job of running the nation's businesses, the tools of production come more into the control of the government and not of the people. Already in this country we have people yelling for the government to take over the oil industry, the railroads, the telephone systems, medical treatment, you name it.

When that happens, when the tools of this great industrial nation become the property of government and not of individual owners, those tools will be wasted and abused.

Look at public housing. Buildings built to last thirty years are run-down and ramshackle after five years. They belong to everybody and they belong to nobody. But if I own a tool, and I am going to reap the benefits of its use, you'd better believe I will take care of it and use it well.

The bottom line is this: when the state controls the tools of production, it controls the people. They become slaves. By withholding the tools from them the state can reduce them to the level of primitive man; by saying when and how and for what purposes those tools may be used, it can control the life of every man.

When Fidel Castro took over Cuba he marched in and took control of the means of production. The young people were elated—they had finally overthrown that dirty scoundrel Batista, that capitalistic pig! Now the "people" owned the cane, the plantations, the refineries. All would be sweetness and light. But when the time came to cut the cane—which is hard, dirty work—some of the students said, "Uh, if you don't mind, Fidel, we don't want to cut the cane."

And Fidel said, "Brothers, together we march forward to cut the cane."

And again they said, "But we don't like to cut cane."

So Fidel said, "You *will* cut the cane! You will either cut the cane or go to jail." So they cut the cane. That is the way the economic life of Cuba has been managed ever since, and likewise in other anticapitalistic countries. The standard of living has just kept going down, until there are more and more poor people, not fewer.

The record of history is clear. The free-enterprise system has outperformed, outproduced any other in the world. It has provided more goods for more people, more jobs in better conditions, more wealth for less labor. It has left people free to control their own lives, to produce at the rate they choose, and reap the benefits of their labor.

It is a gift of God to us, and we should understand it, embrace it, and believe in it.

5

When the president of a large industry walks through his plant, the trip often is a sortie into strange and sometimes hostile territory. In the us-against-them atmosphere which exists in many plants, a typical company president walks among his assembly-line workers as a boss among underlings. He is management and they are labor; he wears an expensive suit and they wear work clothes —the contrasts are obvious. He can expect to be greeted with courtesy, with distant respect, but rarely with warmth and almost never with affection.

A visitor who walks through the Amway

plant in Ada, Michigan, with Rich DeVos should prepare to witness a scene radically different from all that. It is a study in person-to-person warmth flowing both ways between employer and employee.

DeVos moves casually from one part of the gigantic plant to the next, calling out to employees by name, asking about a sick relative here, a new car there. And everywhere he goes he is greeted with wide grins, just-us-folks banter, and volleys of "Hi, Rich," that pour out toward him so naturally and so unselfconsciously from workers of every description that it is positively startling. Young and old, skilled technicians and common laborers, they literally come off the assembly lines to shake his hand and say hello. One feels that these people genuinely like him, that he is more their leader than their boss, and, to some, more a friend than anything else. They seem oblivious to the apparent differences between them and him, perhaps more sensitive to some bond more basic than those differences.

As for DeVos, there is no doubt that he likes them—earnestly, deeply likes them. They are his kind of people, decent and hard-working, and it is clear that he respects them and enjoys being among them.

A gray-haired lady, very short and matronly, looks up from her stool where she is checking the caps on aerosol cans. She recognizes the man standing behind her, breaks suddenly into a smile, and grabs his hand in her own. "You get back up there to that office and get to work, Rich DeVos!" she says, with the mock authority of a staunch mother spooning chicken soup into a reluctant boy. "You and me, we've got to keep this thing rolling!"

And they all seem to feel just that way: you and me, Rich DeVos, you and me have got to keep this thing rolling! And so they do!

BELIEVE!

... in Human Dignity

There is a line from an old song that declares that love "makes the world go 'round." At the risk of sounding hopelessly antiromantic, I would like to revise that line slightly: it is respect that makes the world go 'round. The most important commodity in the world is respect for the individual man.

When I say "respect for the individual man," I mean it in terms of specific, day-to-day attitudes and behavior, not respect for man in some abstract sense of "mankind," but an active, daily awareness of the worth and value of every man, regardless of his situation or station in life, color, creed, or whatever else. I believe that every man on earth is a creature of God, that he is here for a purpose, and that he is worthy of my respect as a human being.

The thing that stands in the way of respect for all God's children is the whole system of pigeonholes and categories into which we push people. We talk about a man according to whether he went to this school or that school, has this degree or that degree, works at this job or another job, according to the car he drives, or the house he lives in, or the accent of his voice. And too often we are so busy relating to him in these little air-tight categories that we never get around to seeing him as a fellow creature on this planet, a brother under the skin, a human individual of worth and destiny. Respect—that is the key. And it is difficult to have real respect for a man if I can only see the cut of his clothes or the color of his money.

We have these sacred labels that we worship. This job is "professional" and that one is not. This person is worthy and that one is disadvantaged. Things such as higher education have emerged as a kind of national mania, so that a person is hardly considered worthy of notice unless he has a college degree. We seem to say, "I don't want to know who you are, what you can do, what the condition of your heart is, what strengths you have, or what obstacles you have overcome —first I want to see your college degree!"

Another category system that has grown equally out of proportion to its real importance is money. It is possible for a worthless fool to have money—just as it is possible for him to get a college degree. Other things are often more important in judging a man than either of these, but too often people are shoved to the background without a chance to show their real worth unless they have money or a college education. They feel like the comedian Rodney Dangerfield, whose trademark is the complaint, "I don't get no respect!" And they have every right to feel that way.

A couple of years ago I was at a symposium on vocational education held by the governor of a northern state. I sat through the meeting all day with men who had doctor's degrees and great experience in higher education; and all day long I heard a stream of comments which showed a deep, pervasive, perhaps even unintentional disrespect for the out-of-work laborer—the very men whom these experts were supposed to be trying to help. I heard lines like this one: "Well, I hope through vocational education we can make these men good citizens." Or, "Maybe at least we can make a good carpenter out of him." Or one of the experts would say, "Well, he would still be *just* a plumber, but. . . ."

Finally I was tired of hearing it. I happened to be the speaker that night, and I opened my remarks by saying, "Gentlemen, with all humility, I would like to say that unless you can develop some respect for the men you're trying to educate, you'd better stop trying to get the job done. You're looking down your noses from your Ph.D. towers and somehow you're trying to find some little niche in society for the poor fellow who isn't bright enough, in your opinion, to get a college degree."

Make no mistake about it, I am all for college education and all for people having lots of money and all for every kind of advancement that anyone can make. But I don't think we should draw up this set of categories and say, in effect, to 100 million Americans, "Since you don't have any of these traditional symbols of success, you are nothing." We have Ph.D.s working for us in the Amway Corporation, chemists and lawyers and computer experts. I recognize the value of their training and their expertise. I salute the kid who scratches and claws and digs his way through college and graduate school and becomes a doctor or a scientist or whatever. But I don't think that he is one bit better than the fifteen hundred honest, hardworking men and women who run the machinery, push the brooms, and do the production-line labor back in the plant. I respect the truck driver who does his thing well.

I resent anyone who says about a non-professional worker, "He is *just* a mechanic," or "*just* a salesman," or *just* anything—he is a warm, giving, highly complex human being, cast in the image of God Himself, who is doing his job with pride and competence. He is the backbone of this country; he is the guy who gets the job done; he is the unsung hero of our whole society—and when I think of all he has accomplished, I practically burst with pride in his achievement and respect for what he is.

One summer my family and I were living at a cottage, and we had a garbage man who was the best garbage man I have ever seen in my life. He was fantastic. He was there at half-past six in the morning; you could set your clock by him. He didn't throw the trash can, didn't heave it in the general direction of the truck and hope it got there. And after he emptied the cans, he didn't sling the lids at them and see how close they came; he always put the lids carefully back in place. He knew the people were sleeping so he worked quietly, did everything neatly and quickly, then drove on to the next cottage.

One morning I got up, pulled my pants on, and watched him come down the road. Half-past six in the morning. When he came to my house, I said, "Hey, I just wanted to tell you what a nice job you're doing." He didn't speak; he just looked at me and walked away. He didn't even answer.

The next week I got up and waited for him again. I watched as he loaded my trash, then I said, "You know, you do a wonderful job. I've never seen a guy tend to his work so well."

He looked at me and asked, "Hey man, are you just now coming in or already going out?" And I answered that I had gotten up to tell him he was doing a good job. He just shook his head and walked away.

I waited for him a third week because I was leaving for the rest of the summer. When he came I said, "I still want to tell you how much I appreciate what you do." And finally he lit up with a big smile.

He said, "You know something? I've been hauling garbage for twelve years. You know, in twelve years nobody has ever told me they appreciated what I was doing. My boss has never told me I do a good job. Nobody has ever said thank you!" He smiled, shook his head again as if he didn't quite believe it, and walked back to his truck.

What an example of a man who deserves respect and rarely gets it! As president of a company, I am told every day what a great job I am doing with this and that. Whether I am doing particularly well or not, I get my ego stroked and my vanity inflated. When a doctor or a professor or a politician does his job well, the praises ring in his ears. He is practically smothered with respect. But this garbage man has worked hard to do his job well for twelve years without ever a word of encouragement or thanks. And still he and millions of workers like him have it said of them by half-grown adolescents, status-conscious relatives, and new-rich neighbors, "Well, he's *just* a garbage man."

The average, ordinary, common American individual, despite his problems and his shortcomings, is worthy of respect as an individual and a productive citizen. Sure, we have problems. Sure, there is crime and welfare chiseling and dishonest dealing. Sure, there are lazy people who won't go to work and who can't be depended upon. But 80 million people went to work today! The country's plants operated today. The banks and stores were open today. All that money was handled by people who are still trustworthy and dependable. You can pick up the phone and there is someone there to get you through to the Fiji Islands or London or any place in the world. People all over the country got to work today, and were waiting there, in the restaurants and drugstores and airplanes and schools, to serve you. Some of them were sick. Some were hung over. Some had sick children. But they were there. The whole world of commerce and industry, banking, finance, hospitals, police forces, service organizations, all operated today. Think of all the alarm clocks that were set, all those who had to arrange to have gas in the tank or a bicycle by the door or to catch that old subway—that somebody else had to drive. Think of all the school buses that ran back and forth across this country in the snow or across the desert or in a driving rain.

Thousands of production lines operated today, and you'll have their goods on your table or on your kid's feet in a few weeks. You turned on the radio or TV and there was someone to tell you the time and play some music for you. People are waiting in tens of thousands of gas stations to pump gas into your car to get you where you are going.

I'm telling you—it's a fast-moving, highly efficient society we live in, and the people who work hard to keep it moving are to be saluted!

I have reflected for many years on the subject of leadership, or the qualities that make a man a good leader, and I have concluded that this thing of respect for other men is the first item on the list. If I had to train a man to take my job overnight, I would forget about trying to teach him the details of the Amway business and spend my time telling him how important it is for him to respect the people working with him and for him. Many people aspire to positions of leadership without realizing that real leadership begins with respect for people. It cannot be gained by talent, intelligence, or hard work alone. Without respect for the people one is to lead, it is impossible to be an effective leader.

Everyone wants to be chief. Not many people realize that the man who becomes a great leader and wins the respect and affection of many followers usually has a respect for his followers which is as deep and real as their respect for him.

Leadership is not something that can be conferred or granted. A man is not a leader until his people accept him as their leader. He can be their boss, their master, but he is still not their leader. A man can gain control over people by being arbitrarily placed over them, or by various authoritarian means. But leadership is more than having authority over people, more than doing the technically correct thing—it is being the person whom people want to follow. The world is filled with persons who have become managers of men, but real leaders are difficult to find. Leadership implies getting the job done through people, and that process requires mutual respect.

Somehow people know when a person respects them for what they are. People will always follow that kind of leader. Respect may be communicated in different ways, but it will invariably be communicated if it is

there. In World War II the United States
had two generals who were greatly different
from each other: Eisenhower and Patton.
Ike's image was that of a kind, gentle leader;
Patton was considered harsh and demanding. But even though Patton was rough and
hard-nosed, he respected the GIs under his
command as competent fighting men. That
respect for them, however gruffly communicated, made him a great leader. Respect for
one's followers does not mean softness or
lack of demands. It means a genuine faith in
them as individuals who can and will get the
job done. If a man knows that his leader has
faith in him to do the job, he will usually do
whatever is humanly possible to measure up.

My own particular "thing" has always
been salesmanship. I have been involved in
sales all my life, and I am always amazed to
see how many people look down their noses
as salesmanship as a worthy occupation. So
few people have respect for salesmen that
eventually the salesman has no respect for
himself. He is embarrassed about what he
does, intimidated by that sneering "Oh,
you're *just* a salesman" stuff. As stated
earlier, there are two hundred thousand independent Amway distributors working for
themselves. As a leader of those people my

first job is to communicate the respect that I genuinely feel, and hope that my respect will rub off on them and what they are doing. A man who believes he is just a crummy old salesman will usually act like a crummy old salesman. He will not be happy, and he will not sell very much, either.

In this day of rapid proliferation of college degrees and obsession with social status, it takes a guy who really has his head together to say simply, "I am a salesman," and not let a lack of respect from others affect him. Why? Because lots of folks think they are too good to sell. They have forgotten that every dollar that is made in America is made because somebody somewhere sold something. Sales generate all the income there is, whether it is the sale of a product or a service or whatever. I was fortunate enough to grow up in a home in which salesmanship was not looked down on, and I've never had to swallow my pride in order to sell something.

Listen to people talk about selling sometime. Their most frequent lines are, "Oh, I just hate to have to try to sell something," or "It just kills me to have to try to sell anything to someone." Do you know what the problem is? Pride. Plain and simple pride of people who hate to ask people to buy, because down deep they have no respect for the art of selling.

On top of that general disrespect for salesmanship, our Amway distributors have to combat the added contempt shown for the person-to-person salesman. I've had people say to me before, "Oh, Amway. You guys are in that direct-selling deal." My answer: Sure we are! We are in the personal-service business. We happen to think that personal service beats making the customer stand in line. We don't apologize for it. I respect the man who is in a business where the customers need not beat their way through traffic, park way out in a crowded parking lot, and run through the rain or snow to get their goods. I respect the man who brings it to their doors, and if he respects the value of his own service he is to be praised and not put down for it.

I believe it is high time for us to get off each other's backs and out of each other's hair, quit the petty sniping and fussing and bickering about this group and that group, and get on with the business of making a better life for ourselves and our children. It is time to quit tearing each other down, to quit singing, "My job is better than your job," to quit playing one-upmanship between

this and that group, and start building one
another up. You can try to understand my
situation, look at the good in me, give me
credit for a bit of intelligence and basic
decency—in short, you can give mè *respect*
—and I will be a better person for it. And I,
on the other hand, can channel the same
human respect back to you, and you will be
a better person for it. God wants us to get
along that way, to be good for each other, to
build each other up, and it all starts with
respect.

When was the last time you took five
minutes to say thank you in a note to that
schoolteacher who wipes your kid's nose and
helps him find his boots when they are lost
and puts up with his racket and his rowdi-
ness? When was the last time you thanked
the policeman who gave you a speeding ticket,
thanked him for his hard work with a hundred hassles every day? When was the last
time a cop got that kind of respect from
you? When was the last time you expressed
gratitude to that usher at your church who
has done his job for twenty years without
complaining or shirking, for no pay and little
thanks? When did you last write a note to a
candidate for political office who ran and
lost, just to tell him how much you respect

his willingness to put it all on the line to make democracy work? How often do you tell the waitress at that restaurant where you get coffee every morning that you appreciate how hard she works every day to keep her customers happy?

Think of all those people who are your friends, your customers, clients or colleagues, those people who rub shoulders with you every day, whose hard work or friendship or special skills make your life better. How many of those people *know* how much you respect them for what they are, how much you respect the way they live their lives and do their jobs? You do respect them; you do need them and admire them in a thousand small ways. So tell them. Show them. Let that respect for them show. Turn it loose and let it show. It's what makes the world go 'round!

6

In the early days of the Amway organization, Rich DeVos was asked to make a speech to a group of women accountants. He was expected to speak on a topic related to business, but on that particular occasion, he recalls, there was another subject which for some reason seemed more important to him. He had grown weary of going to PTA meetings, Kiwanis Club luncheons, or wherever groups of people got together to hear speakers talk about the sad shape the country was in.

It was the early 1960s, and the Cold War was still on with Russia and the Communist countries. The Cuban missile crisis was only a few months behind, and Americans everywhere were gloomy and pessimistic. So that day at the meeting of women accountants, DeVos put aside his business topic and spent the hour extolling the virtues of the United States of America.

That was the beginning of DeVos's now well-known role as an outspoken proponent of the American way of life. The off-the-cuff speech to that small women's group soon developed into a speech called "Selling America," which was heard and cheered by literally scores of audiences of all descriptions over the next ten years. It was recorded and sold as a long-play album, and later distributed as a cassette tape. The speech won several awards, including the Alexander Hamilton Award from the Freedoms Foundation.

DeVos does many things well, but he is probably at his best as a public speaker. He crisscrosses the country by private jet, speaking at occasions ranging from small high-school graduations to gigantic sales rallies which fill massive auditoriums. Virtually without exception his effect on audiences is electrifying. In the words of one of his aides, "He wipes 'em out!"

DeVos almost always speaks without

notes. His approach is usually informal; often he leaves the platform to get closer to the people, sometimes engaging members of the audience in dialogue as he speaks.

DeVos is reluctant to discuss his obvious charisma as an onstage speaker. "Aw, most of what I say I've borrowed from other people anyway," he declares. Maybe so. But whether he is explaining the Amway sales plan or preaching free enterprise to the National Association of Manufacturers, he leaves those who hear him with an experience that they don't easily forget.

BELIEVE!

. . . in America

Recently a gentleman in Grand Rapids, Michigan, decided to sell his house. He called a local realtor and asked him to take the listing. The realtor returned to his office and prepared an ad to put in the paper telling about the features of this house. That evening the gentleman who had listed his house was reading the paper and looking, of course, to see if it was being advertised. He read the ad, and read it again and again. Suddenly he got up from his chair and went to the telephone. He called the realtor and told him to cancel the listing. The realtor was completely surprised and asked, "What's the matter? What caused you to suddenly change your mind? Only yesterday you wanted to sell your house and now you want me to cancel it. Why the change?"

The man's answer was very simple. He said, "After I read your ad, I suddenly realized I already live in the house I always wanted to live in."

This story is typical of many Americans who already live in a land that gives them everything they could hope for in this world, and yet they do not realize it. In the early 1950s thousands of our young men fought a war in Korea. A disturbing thing happened there which had never occurred before in the history of the United States. About seven thousand of our young men who were taken captive by the Chinese Communists sat it out. They made no attempt to escape; they just decided to take the candy and cigarettes and the food, play it cool, and not get involved. They gave up their freedom without even a contest.

A psychiatrist by the name of Meyer interviewed over a thousand of these men upon their return. His conclusion was that the young men weren't convinced that America was worth standing up for anymore.

I couldn't help but recall famous escapes of history—General MacArthur's escape from Corregidor, the hundreds of escapes by American servicemen during World War II, and the dramatic accounts from Vietnam.

If the question were put to those men, "Why did you take the risk? Why did you gamble to get out of prison?" the answer would be simple. They would say, "Because we wanted to be free." And now, here were groups of Americans who weren't so sure America was worth the price.

The Communists told those boys how wonderful their system of socialism was, that it was far superior to America's capitalism and our men sat there and listened. Some believed, and many more doubted, and others weren't so sure anymore about The American Way.

I believe in America. In a time when flag-waving is discouraged, I don't apologize at all for an old-fashioned, hand-over-heart, emotional brand of patriotism. I believe that America is the greatest country in the world, with the richest past, the brightest future, and the most exciting present of any nation anywhere.

If one compares America as it is with America as it might potentially be, it is inevitable that there is plenty to fuss about. Are there problems in America? Sure there are. There is too much poverty, too much crime, too much alcoholism and divorce. There is inflation and recession and an emotional hangover still lingering from the war in Vietnam. There are plenty of problems, and only a fool would deny that they exist.

I remember when I was a kid in Sunday school the teacher always warned us not to take a Scripture verse out of its context in the Bible. When you study the Bible you take the whole chapter, the whole passage—because if you just pick a verse here and a verse there you can make the Bible prove any point you like. Too many people look at America like that. They pick a problem here and a little defect there and pretty soon they build a whole case around those few faults. They take the problems out of context and preach sermons on how America is going to the dogs!

The worst thing about such distortion is that the people who do it are often very influential. They have an audience among the nation's young people. Our kids get all hung up on some minor defects and lose their perspective; they lose the perspective necessary to balance the debits and the credits and see the whole picture of what America is like. The only way to keep the perspective straight is to ask the second question, "Compared to what?" It is when America is compared with other countries that a true picture is most apparent.

Many of us have stopped talking about the wonderful things that free enterprise has given to all of us. Let me quote a few statistics, a listing of the assets of America, and a comparison of where we stand as opposed to Communist Russia, which attempts to tell people all across the world that their system is superior to ours. It may be better for a handful of leaders, but when we look at the people who live under that system, we find them living in situations which by our standards constitute extreme poverty. Let me give you a few figures for comparison.

In order to enjoy the glories of the present Soviet system, and to bring our resources to their level, we would have to abandon half of our steel capacity, one-half of our petroleum capacity, destroy three of every five hydroelectric plants, and get along on a third of our volume of natural gas.

We would have to rip up thirteen of every fourteen miles of our paved highways, and two of every three miles of our main-line railroad tracks.

We'd scrap nineteen out of every twenty cars and trucks, destroy over two thousand colleges and universities and burn 85 percent of our museums.

We would cut our living standard by two-thirds, destroy 50 million television sets, ten out of every eleven telephones, seven of every ten single-family houses; and then we would have to put about sixty-eight million people back on the farms.

A graphic example of direct competition between the two countries was the "space race." Back in the 1950s the Russians shot the first sputnik satellite into space. We suddenly saw in headlines all across America that we had lost the space race: RUSSIA LEADS—AMERICA ISN'T EVEN CLOSE. RUSSIA WILL DOMINATE THE WORLD BY DOMINATING SPACE. Newspaper after newspaper across the world told us we were doomed because Russia had gone first into space, and we weren't even close to having anything going.

But when the American people with American ingenuity and determination put their minds to the job, we became the ones to walk on the moon. We were the ones who have been there and back. We landed a vehicle on it. Listen to the rest of the statistics: Sixteen years after the first sputnik, we had twenty-seven manned space flights compared to Russia's eighteen. We had twenty-one multiman flights compared to their nine. We had put sixty men in space, they had put thirty-two there. We had nine space walks, they had one. We had seven space linkups, they had only two. We had been to the moon four times, landed twice, and come back. They haven't put a man on it yet.

But let's forget statistics and production data for a while and talk about something much closer to the real secret of American superiority. America has always been the land of plenty—plenty of men, plenty of resources, plenty of all the necessities of life.

But when we study the history of this land we realize that it was not immigration or climate or resources alone that made America great. We see that there is another factor to be reckoned with when the American nation is judged. That factor leaves its traces in a thousand history books and millions of lives. It can be found every day of the year from Maine to Miami, from the chalets of Vermont to the ranch houses of Arizona, from the gentleman farmer of Virginia to the bartender in San Diego. This factor is the faith which binds us all together and makes of us one people. It is the spirit of America.

The spirit of America is an intangible

thing and is extremely difficult to define. It has its roots in a political philosophy, but it is more than that. One may regard it as commonly shared regional traits, but it is something more than that. It smacks strongly of nationalism and patriotism, but it goes deeper still than that.

The spirit of America is all these things lumped into one. It is the thing that sets Americans apart from all other people of the world and marks them as children of destiny. This intangible quality is expressed in the inscription on the Statue of Liberty:

... Give me your tired, your poor,
Your huddled masses yearning to
breathe free. ...

Here it is! Here is the essence of the American spirit! "... yearning to breathe free. ..." Yearning to taste the fullness of life, yearning to kick off restraint and plot an independent course, yearning to stretch dormant muscles and operate at full capacity, yearning to tear down old barns and build new ones, to cast off security and gamble on the long chance, to defy precedent and seek adventure.

"... yearning to breathe free. ..." Free

to be an individual, free to be a tycoon or a gutter bum, to be everything or nothing; free to follow the inner voice, to believe or doubt, to agree or disagree; free to wear the blue or the gray, to march with Grant or with Lee.

That call of freedom went forth from a rugged wilderness, and Europe and Asia and Africa sent their sons of adventure to hew out a new society in a land of forests and savages. They came lean and hungry, tired of tyranny, eager to find new lives. And when they found that freedom of mind and body they sought, they assumed a reckless self-confidence that knew no defeat. They tore the concept of inferiority to shreds, made a shambles of the negative approach, and threw the words "second best" out of their vocabularies. Out of this came the spirit of America, and with this spirit they built our nation and forged our heritage.

Of course, there have always been those who have underestimated and discredited the power of the American spirit. One of the first of these was an English king named George. He is remembered by Britons today as the man who lost the American colonies. Another man who misjudged this spirit was a Mexican named Santa Anna. He died in poverty in Mexico City with memories of the Alamo and San Jacinto still coming back to haunt him. And then there was that man called Hitler, who scoffed at the American spirit one year and died in a Berlin bunker the next.

In this day of statistical analysis, when the "cold fact" is glorified, it is tempting to scoff and smirk when a thing such as spirit is introduced into a political problem. And now, when the United States finds itself in critical times, all the alarmists and cynics around the globe come to the conclusion that all is lost and the democratic ideals of Americanism are about to be destroyed. Of those who despair and sneer at the American spirit, history would ask a few questions:

Where were they when a handful of painted New Englanders dumped the king's tea into the briny Boston harbor? Where were they when a thin, ragged line of angry colonists stood off the British army at Bunker Hill? Where were they when Nathan Hale flung into the face of the British army his pride in dying for his country? Where were they when the cotton bales of New Orleans spat out the fire and thunder of Andrew Jackson's fury? Where were they when brave men locked arms at the Alamo? Where were

they when Johnny came marchin' home?
Where were the skeptics when fever-ridden
engineers scraped out the Panama Canal?
Where were they when the trees of Argonne
Forest shook with Yankee gunfire? Where
were they when Lindbergh flew the Atlantic,
when Peary crossed the North Pole, when
Edison destroyed darkness with a light bulb,
when Neil Armstrong kicked up dust on the
moon?

The skeptics have always been there, and
still America has always moved ahead, solv-
ing its problems, coping with new demands,
always showing resilience and toughness
when the chips were down. Sure, these are
difficult times, as there have been difficult
times before. But one thing can be counted
on: in the crunch, the American spirit never
breaks!

As a final point, I would submit to you
that the real strength of America is its religious tradition. I am concerned that too
many people have lost sight of the fact that
America is what it is today because God has
blessed this land. Too many people today
are willing to act as if God had nothing what-
soever to do with it. They don't even want
to mention Him anymore. This country was
built on a religious heritage, and we'd better

get back to it. We had better start telling people that faith in God is the real strength of America! It is true, as the Bible states, that faith comes through hearing, which demands that we begin telling of God's grace to this country.

When this country was founded, the Pilgrims offered prayer on that first Thanksgiving Day. Even to this day, as a continuation of that heritage, the United States Congress in Washington, D.C., opens with prayer at every session. Whenever I pick up a dollar bill or any piece of change I see the words "In God We Trust." This, too, is a part of that heritage, a recognition of the fact that in God is the strength of America.

We have always believed in this country that man was created in the image of God. As such he was given talents and responsibilities and was instructed to use them to make the world a better place. This is the really great thing of America, and this is what contrasts with everything that Russia and many other societies attempt to achieve. The strength of America lies in the faith of its people, who, by their efforts and their faith, have made the United States what it is.

It is time all of us began to sell America, to tell others of her assets so that they will be inspired to greater effort and renewed faith.

Perhaps the man who summed it up best was Carlos P. Romulo, soldier, statesman, and Philippine patriot, who served with General MacArthur in World War II and played a leading role in creating the United Nations. He was the Philippine ambassador to this country for many years, and a former president of the UN General Assembly. When he left America for the last time, he said this:

I am going home, America—farewell. For seventeen years, I have enjoyed your hospitality, visited every one of your fifty states. I can say I know you well. I admire and love America. It is my second home. What I have to say now in parting is both a tribute and a warning: Never forget, Americans, that yours is a spiritual country. Yes, I know that you are a practical people. Like others, I have marveled at your factories, your skyscrapers and your arsenals. But underlying everything else is the fact that America began as a God-loving, God-fearing, God-worshiping people, knowing that there is a spark of the Divine in each one of us. It is this respect for the dignity of the human spirit which makes America invincible. May it always endure.

And so I say again in parting, thank you, America, and farewell. May God keep you always—and may you always keep God.

7

Into the building of glass and gleaming steel.
Through the large, high-ceilinged rotunda
and up wide, winding stairs to a second-floor
landing. And then past layers of secretaries
and offices and finally into the office of Rich
DeVos.

It is tastefully and expensively done, as
one would expect of the quarters of a corporate president, but it is not the furniture or
the sweeping plate-glass view or the opu-
lence that is interesting: it is the walls,
a veritable smorgasbord of memorabilia,
awards, and photographs, a blend of personal and professional things that talk loudly

of man who inhabits this space. Carpet and furniture and draperies can be planned by interior decorators, ordered by phone, and installed by workmen, never revealing a thing about the man. But here on the walls are clues that draw the observant visitor to look and ponder like an archaeologist over hieroglyphs in an ancient tomb.

There are awards of every type, recognition of humanitarian and philanthropic ventures, citations honoring public service and that famous "Selling America" speech, scrolls proclaiming honorary citzenship in a variety of cities and states. There is a plaque of appreciation from the Dallas Cowboys football team, a photograph of DeVos arm-in-arm with then-Vice-President Gerald Ford, a sketch of him and his partner drawn by Norman Rockwell. And there are the personal touches, photographs which show his wife and children, handsome and suntanned, and he among them, all six faces wearing those easy, honest smiles seen on families who enjoy being together.

It is all here, a rich, diverse record of a highly successful man.

But there is something else on that wall which perhaps tells more about the man than any of the awards and trophies. It is a

motto, simply inscribed and framed, hanging quietly among the more spectacular ob-
jects of color and gold. DeVos is not a man
given to slogans, yet it is there, and one
feels that its message, or one like it, has
spoken powerfully to him over the years. It
reads:

Press on.
Nothing in the world can take the place
of persistence. Talent will not; nothing
is more common than unsuccessful men
with talent. Genius will not; unre-
warded genius is almost a proverb. Education alone will not; the world is full
of educated derelicts. Persistence and
determination alone are omnipotent.

BELIEVE!

... in the Power of Persistence

When our children were small, we often read them the story of *The Little Engine That Could*. Over the years, thousands of young people have heard this story and caught its message: There is no substitute for a determined belief that hard work and effort will always pay off.

If I had to select one quality, one personal characteristic that I regard as being most highly correlated with success, whatever the field, I would pick the trait of persistence. Determination. The will to endure to the end, to get knocked down seventy times and get up off the floor saying, "Here goes number seventy-one!"

Of course, some people confuse persistence with stubbornness. They think determination and mule-headedness are one and the same. They are not. One can be foolishly and nonproductively stubborn. He can be stubborn about almost anything from insisting that water is not wet to demanding that time stand still. Stubbornness often exists for its own sake, with no relationship to reality or function. Persistence, on the other hand, is stubbornness with a purpose. It is determination with a goal in mind. One dictionary defines persistence as "a tenacious will to exist, a hardy struggle against odds."

The thing that elevates persistence above the level of stubbornness is that persistence flows from a decision that has been made toward a goal that is in sight. Random, aimless stubbornness is an annoying quality, but persistence that follows a decision in an individual's life can be the single most important characteristic in his chances of success or failure.

I had an experience early in my high-school days that taught me the value of making tough decisions and persisting in them. My first year in high school I attended Grand Rapids Christian High School, a private school. I really didn't think a lot about

the fact that I was going to a private school,
or that it was costing my dad lots of hard-
earned money. I was just there. So I chased
the girls and I goofed off. I was not the best
student in the world, so I'm the kind of
person who has to apply, and I didn't apply!
I didn't actually flunk anything, although
the only way I scraped through Latin was by
promising never to take it again.

My dad was pretty unhappy about my
poor grades that first year, so he said, "Well,
son, if that's the way it's going to be, if
you're going to goof off anyway, I'm not
going to pay this money to send you to
private school." So the next year I went to
a public school. I didn't like it there, and
when my third year of high school rolled
around, I told Dad that I intended to go
back to Christian High School. "Humph,"
he said, "if you go back there I hope you
realize that you are going to have to pay for
it yourself." That really laid it on the line. I
could stay at the public school, or I could
switch back to Christian High. The decision
was mine to make. But if I went to the school
that I preferred, I was going to have to be
determined enough to pay the freight. I
thought it over. I figured out the cost. I had
a job at a gas station, and I thought I could

make enough money to pay the tuition as I went, so I said, "I'm going back to Christian High School. I'll pay the bill myself."

That was the first time in my life I had ever made a decision of that magnitude, a decision that had to be followed up, that had to be backed up by persistence and determination. I look back on that autumn day as an important time in my growth. It was a point in my life where, for the first time, I not only decided to do something which I chose to do, but I was willing to back it up by saying, "This is the price I'll pay to get it." (To finish that story, my parents eventually helped with my tuition, after seeing that I was serious in my choice.)

It takes a decision to turn persistence loose and let it operate. Some people will never know whether they have any real capacity for determination, because they will never put themselves on the line and commit themselves to a decision that they know might require sleepless nights and long, hard days of work.

It is amazing how much of our lives is determined not by big decisions, but by little ones that pile up on us until the big ones are automatically made. The average person usually says that the biggest decision he ever made was the day he decided to get married. I've had a lot of men tell me that, and I laugh, because I have never met a fellow yet who decided to get married. What happened, you see, was that he made a little decision to ask a certain girl out. And then he tried it again. And things just gradually moved on from there and the next thing he knew he was married and had a family and he had a job and so on. Another "big" decision is the job a man works at. But usually he didn't make any kind of major decision. It just happened to be a handy thing at the time it came up, and the firm had an opening, and so he took it and he couldn't afford to quit and on he goes.

It takes real courage to make a major decision; to really take a look at one's situation and dare to grab things by the throat and make a tough, important decision. But that is the only way to get on the track toward goals that really matter. Ben Jonson, one of the great English writers, once said, "What is written without effort is generally read without pleasure." That is the way it is with decisions. Very often those things that are decided without pain and commitment, without counting the cost and taking a risk, are generally pursued without passion or persistence. Life just rocks along, and things stay pretty much the same as they have always been.

Once you select a goal that is really important to you and make a decision to pursue it, the next step is to make up your mind before you set out toward it that it is going to require lots of hard work. You know that and you accept it. You make up your mind before you start that sacrifice is part of the package. In the Amway business we tell thousands of people every year about the opportunity to get ahead by developing a second career in direct selling. But we never try to make it sound easy. If a guy is looking for a shortcut to prosperity, we don't want him. When you set out to get that promotion, or to earn that degree, or to build that vacation house, or to learn that new skill, you may as well know that an eight-hour day won't be good enough anymore. If you are afraid to work more than eight hours, don't even start out to improve your situation. If you are a nut about television and you just *must* watch it, then forget about that extra goal. If bowling is the center of your life and you just can't give up three nights a week at the neighborhood lanes, then go ahead and resign yourself to stay pretty much where you are in life.

If all these things are important to you, that's fine. There is nothing wrong with those things. But if you are so hooked on them that you are never going to go after those things you've always talked about, then at least stop complaining and envying the other fellow, and try to enjoy what you have. Go ahead and do all the things that fill up your time and that never force you to push yourself and improve yourself. But don't cry because other people have more than you have.

When you find a goal and have the commitment to work for it even when you feel like taking it easy, then all that is left is to persist! Keep on keeping on. Take the peaks and the valleys in stride and roll on toward that goal. Don't let the odds that are against you or the obstacles that fall in your path dissuade you for a moment. Persist. That is the key. Get your eyes so firmly on the goal that you don't have time to listen to all the reasons that you can't make it.

One of the most inspiring stories I have ever heard was the account of how a man named Robert Manrey took a 13½-foot boat and sailed it across the Atlantic Ocean. If he had asked me before he left, I would have told him to stay home. There was no way he could make it. But fortunately, he didn't ask me. He fell overboard six times; he had to tie himself to the mast to keep from being washed away in storms, but he made it. He got across safely and became quite famous in sailing circles for it.

The experiences Jay Van Andel and I had in the first few years of the Amway Corporation remind me somewhat of that sailor. If we had listened to anyone, we would never have begun. We are often asked if we visualized a company of the present size from the outset. The answer is an emphatic *no!* Neither of us ever had a master plan, a grand scheme, a dream of a quarter-billion-dollar-sales-per-year company.

I'll never forget the night we decided to have a go at it. We were students at Calvin College at the time, and we were in Florida together for the Christmas vacation. We were lying in a bed in a little house in Florida, bursting with ideas for getting started in business. So we made the decision that night: Let's quit talking about it and *do* it! Let's go on with it! Let's just *charge!*

We had a simple goal: to build a successful business for ourselves. We were prepared to make whatever sacrifices were necessary to meet that goal. And we persisted. When we passed one point, only then did we look ahead to the next one. When we had the first million dollars in gross sales, then we thought about the second million. When we outgrew the first building we built another one. And gradually we saw what is now the international Amway Corporation develop. Persistence—not brilliant planning or blind luck or clever promotion—has been the key.

I remember one night in Lansing, Michigan, Jay and I had a big sales meeting. That was in the early days. It was really going to be a dandy meeting! We had been on radio with big ads, had put notices in the papers. All day long we collared people and passed out brochures, revving up for the big meeting. We had an auditorium with two hundred seats, and that night two people showed up! Did you ever make a rock-'em-sock-'em sales speech to two people in a room with two hundred seats in it? And then drive home at two o'clock in the morning because you couldn't afford to pay those motel rates? In situations like that, night after night, you do one of two things. Either you give up, or you persist. We persisted.

We started the business in our basements,

but one thing led to another, and we recruited more and more people to sell our two products. So we bought a garage. Not a big place—just a sixty-by-forty-foot space. We bought two acres and almost passed up a chance to buy two more because we thought we would never need it. We decided to get it anyway, thinking we could use it for a parking lot. Things just grew and grew. We tried everything that caught our fancy. If it worked we made it a part of our product line. If it didn't, we discarded it. Trial and error. We tried selling fallout shelters, until we discovered how much fun it was to dig a hole and bury one of those things in the ground! We sold battery additives, and the batteries froze. We sold electric generators. We even sold water softeners for a while. I remember clearly the night that we decided against staying with the water-softener business. A woman called me at two o'clock in the morning to tell me her water softener was making a funny noise! We learned the hard way!

If I could wish for any person in the United States a single quality to secure for him success in life, I would not grant to him a massive intellect or a well-coordinated, athletic body. I would not wish for him glib-

ness of tongue or personal popularity. I
would not bless him with physical attractive-
ness or talent. I would wish for him the
ability and the will to persist toward whatever his goal.

I enjoy sailing. There are many lessons to
be learned on the water, and one of them is
that there is no such thing as a bad wind. All
winds are good winds if one knows what to
do with them. Any breeze will take a sailing
ship to its destination if it is properly
handled. In life, when the foul winds blow,
that is a lesson to remember. A few lines of
verse by Ella Wheeler Wilcox make the
point:

One ship drives east another drives west
With the selfsame winds that blow.
'Tis the set of sails
And not the gales
Which tells us the way to go.

Like the winds of the sea are the winds
   of fate,
As we voyage along through life,
'Tis the set of the soul
That decides its goal
And not the calm or the strife.

8

Rich DeVos has just finished a speech in Montreal, Canada. The crowd, a larger one than expected, filled the hotel meeting hall to capacity with scores of listeners standing in the back of the room. DeVos has worked hard in the meeting; he is tired now, and sits wearily in the lobby outside the hall as the session continues inside. He sips a cup of coffee, glad to have a moment to relax before going back into the meeting.

Cautiously, apologetically, a middle-aged man approaches DeVos. He is short and thick-middled, wearing glasses. He is apparently uncomfortable in the presence of De-

Vos, self-conscious and a bit flustered to be so close to a man whom he has previously seen from greater distances. But he has a message to give, and he is determined to deliver it, like a burden off his back, to DeVos.

He is a French-speaking Canadian, and he tries to express himself in short snatches of imperfect English. It is not good enough. The words are just not there, and after "Hello" and "I thank you for being here," his attempt to express himself in the awkward language falters and stops. But he does not give up easily. He has something to say, something that his broken English will not allow him to express, and he is determined not to miss his chance to say it.

In frustration, he stops, sits abruptly beside DeVos, pulls a small card from his pocket, and scrawls a message on it. Finishing, he looks up with wet eyes and hands the card wordlessly to DeVos.

"Mr. DeVos," it reads, "The peoples will be better because of you."

DeVos smiles, embraces him. *"Merci . . .* God bless you." And the man, having said what he came to say, walks without further comment back toward the meeting hall.

BELIEVE!

... in God and His Church

As strongly as I believe in free enterprise, human dignity, accountability, an optimistic outlook, and the other principles already discussed there is one thing in which I believe even more strongly.

I believe in a personal God, in His Son Jesus Christ, and in the mission of His church.

Admittedly, a man's view of God is an extremely personal matter. And his relationship with God is perhaps the most intimate thing in his entire life. I have never been one to intrude my own personal religious convictions into the lives of other persons against their will. Ultimately, however, a man must be willing to declare publicly the faith which he feels in his heart. Without being dogmatic or pushy, he must be willing to share, with whomever will listen, the convictions which he has found important in his own life.

Occasionally people ask me, "Is Amway a Christian organization?" I always answer that it certainly is not. It has lots of wonderful Christian people in it, but an organization cannot be Christian. Only people can be Christian, because Christianity is a person-to-Person thing. It is a one-to-One relationship between an individual and Jesus Christ. I refuse to use the machinery of the Amway Corporation to foist my private convictions on others, and conversely, I do not use the Gospel to promote my business. But I cannot compartmentalize the person I am. I cannot hang my religion on the hat rack as I leave the church on Sunday and pick it up again when I return a week later. I am a Christian by faith and by experience, and in no aspect of my life can I make major decisions or take positions which are not compatible with my discipleship.

I cannot remember a time when I did not believe in God. I had the good fortune of growing up in a Christian family, and I've known the feel of the church pew from my earliest recollection. In high school I began to notice that there was a difference between the company of Christian people and those who had no faith. I was not very analytical at the time, but I knew the general atmosphere among Christians was somehow different. There was a greater warmth, a surer sense of meaning and purpose, more deeply felt interpersonal bonds among those who shared a common Christian faith. I became aware that there were two kinds of people in the world: those who loved God and embraced His church, and those who did not. And I knew that it was with the Christian group that I belonged.

Soon after returning from military service in World War II, I joined the Christian Reformed Church, and I have been a member since that time. But only in the last few years have I really known the excitement and blessing that comes from being a totally involved Christian. For many years I was a fairly typical church member going to worship services, paying my fair share of the church's support, but never making my discipleship a major part of my life. In the last few years, my wife and I have "moved off dead center," to use her words, and it has been an exciting experience to follow God's lead as He has helped us to grow up in Him.

Somehow people seem surprised to hear a corporation president discuss the importance of spiritual things. The stereotype is that the big-business executive is ruthless and mercenary, concerned only with the bottom line, far too preoccupied with material things to care about the things of the Spirit. I cannot imagine a more inaccurate image. There is nothing that can convince a man of the inadequacy of money quite so fast as having some of it! A poor man might go a lifetime with the delusion that if he only had enough money all his problems would disappear. When he acquires a fortune, he discovers just how limited money can be. Money cannot buy peace of mind. It cannot heal ruptured relationships, or build meaning into a life that has none. It cannot relieve guilt or speak to the great agonies of the broken heart.

No one knows this better than the man with money. If he is honest with himself, he knows that all that he has materially comes from the hand of God, and only in combination with worship of that God can his money bring real happiness.

At the same time, material things are not

to be automatically regarded as antispiritual. Many people holler about the evils of materialism as if material things were somehow intrinsically bad. That is an illogical attitude. It makes absolutely no sense to me to make materialism the scapegoat for man's lack of interest in spiritual things. Everything in the world is material. The Bible is material—black ink on paper with leather binding. A minister wears a suit made of material, preaches from a pulpit made of material, through a microphone made of material. Obviously there is nothing wrong with material—out of it God created all things. It is only the excessive love of material things that Scripture condemns.

I believe that material goods were put on this earth for people to enjoy. God does not object to that. The Bible tells us not to worship material things, of course, but it does not tell us not to enjoy the fruits of the earth and man's labor. It is significant that God thought it important to restore to Job all his material wealth after Satan had taken it away. Job was faithful to God, and God apparently wanted him to enjoy not only spiritual blessings but material wealth as well as a reward for that faithfulness. God obviously does not regard material wealth as evil in and of itself.

That is not to say that the pursuit of money may not be a problem for a Christian. Without doubt, a man's money can come between him and God. Money is power. It brings to a man the power to make his day-to-day routine less difficult, to move other men this way or that, to exercise greater control over the conditions under which he lives. And that power can corrupt. If he becomes intoxicated with the power which money brings and forgets that the source of his money is the hand of God, then he becomes arrogantly self-reliant, forgetting that God owns all things, and gives or withholds them at His pleasure. The most effective way for a man to keep his material blessings in true perspective is to remind himself constantly that all of it comes from God.

Sometimes I think about the many people who are smarter, more deserving, more talented than I am, and I ask God, *"Why, Lord, have things worked out this way for me? Why me and not someone else?"* I think of the innumerable little miracles beyond my control which have worked together so beautifully to my benefit, and I can only acknowledge that all I have is truly God's, and for some reason I am His steward over it.

The primary thing is to maintain a sense of dependence on God. That is what humility is all about. But God is as much interested in the attitude of a $150-a-week man toward his money as he is with a millionaire's attitude. The wealthy man has more to account for, more responsibility for the way he uses his surplus, but God is still interested in the state of his heart more than in the shape of his net-worth statement. When He blesses a man materially, He does it for a reason greater than merely that individual's personal comfort, and the man with money must accept accountability for that higher purpose. He can never escape God's requirement that he answer for his use of what he has.

I would not be honest if I didn't admit that on occasions I feel a tinge of guilt for the standard of living that we enjoy here in America. Maybe the word "uneasy" is a better choice. But I don't think there is anything unusual about that. I think that every middle-class American, if he is candid, will admit that he is made uncomfortable when he thinks about the starving children in Biafra, the 200 million people in India who live on less than forty dollars a year, the poverty in Bangladesh, the great needs of people in our own country. Certainly all of us who live in nice homes, drive comfortable automobiles, and eat three square meals a day must feel a bit uneasy when we are confronted with the poverty of much of the world.

But we must remember that a poor man cannot help another poor man. An impoverished nation cannot help another impoverished nation get on its feet. There has always been poverty in the world, and it does not help the situation for men—or nations—of material strength to wallow in some kind of neurotic guilt about that fact. Like any person who has a high standard of living—which includes almost every person reading this book—I can only thank God for His help and vow to be a responsible, generous steward of what I have. In a famous parable that Christ told, a man gave one of his servants five pieces of money, and to another servant He gave only one. He did not demand of the man who was given the five that he redistribute his wealth. He did not want that man to give his five talents to those who had only two or one. Instead he demanded that the man given more money should keep it, use it, enlarge it, and make more with it. The servant that was given one talent sinned by being stingy with what he had been given, and in being afraid to work with it—perhaps even risk it —to make more of it (*see* Matthew 25).

Apart from the problems of greed and arrogance, the other evil associated with money is the sin which occurs when money is gained unfairly, at the expense of others. God does not want any man to be wealthy so much that He would approve of his taking advantage of others. Industry had a bad record on that score in the last century and the first half of the 1900s. No question about it—there were many abuses of the working man, and of the consumer, by certain industries and businesses in the past. I don't want to be overly defensive of big business, or take a naïve, Pollyanna position, but I believe that such abuses are rare today. A great majority of businessmen or industrialists genuinely want to deliver the best product they can at the lowest price, and they want happy employees who are well paid for their work. I cannot buy the image of the big-business leader as a hard-nosed, hard-hearted, rip'-em-off Scrooge who cruelly builds a fortune at the expense of the worker and the public. Over the long haul, businessmen who operate on the basis of greed and manipulation are not successful. Somewhere along the way most of them are done in by their own dishonesty and scheming. There are exceptions, of course, but I still believe that there is a certain justice in the world which rewards goodness and punishes badness.

Can a sensitive young man get to the top of the business world without compromising his Christian commitment? Of course he can! If he remembers that he is responsible to God for both his money and his relationships with other people, he can go to the very top in business without losing an ounce of his love for God or his commitment to Christian brotherhood. And if he does, he can make as great a contribution to the Kingdom of God through his business skills as any minister can do through his theological training or any missionary can do with his medical skills.

After all, can you imagine how the church would do its work without the thousands of committed businessmen who support its programs? Can you imagine a church with nothing but ministers in it? Impossible! And make no mistake about it: the church and its work are important. With all its shortcomings and critics, the church is still a vital institution to the Kingdom of God and to this nation; and for it to do its job, it needs the support of millions of hardworking, turned-on Christians.

The claim that the church is dead and lifeless is not without basis in many cases. There are thousands of congregations which have long ago lost their "first love," abandoned the task of spreading the Gospel and winning new converts, and have become social clubs whose members are going through the motions, primarily for the sake of tradition—and a vague sense that it is the right thing to do. I can understand that, because for many years my wife and I fit that description pretty closely. Our faith was not a personal thing with us; we were not emotionally involved; we were unconcerned about converting the lost and reaching new people with the message of Christ. And that is where many church members in churches of every faith are today.

When those kinds of members fill the pews, the church drifts off on tangents that have little to do with spreading the Gospel. The primary business of the church is not to develop welfare projects, lead in political activism, quibble endlessly over tiny theological issues, and all the other quasi-religious activities with which it gets involved. The work of the church is to tell the Gospel as effectively as possible to as many people as possible. There is nothing wrong with social involvement; it is just not the most important aspect of the church's work. The church has limited resources. It simply cannot solve all the social ills of the world. And so often it becomes so absorbed in that area that it ignores its real purpose. It gets so bogged down in the training sessions and the reaction programs, the dividing of the resources to this program and that program, the quibbling over who will chair what committee, that it gets totally off the track of bringing new people to the Lord.

When the church changes from an organization concerned with evangelism to one which is preoccupied with internal, irrelevant squabbles and "busywork," it follows a pattern often seen in other institutions. I have watched the changes in various institutions for years—churches, companies, homes, even the nation itself—and have seen the same evolution occur over and over. An institution, if it doesn't constantly resist it, inevitably and gradually follows this vitality-draining pattern. There are four stages in the course of these changes: (1) the creating stage; (2) the organizing stage; (3) the defending stage; (4) the stage of "dividing the spoils."

In the *first* stage, someone starts out with a dream, an idea, a burning motivation. It could be a young family setting out to make a good life for itself, a church being organized by a group of new Christians, a business or company with a unique idea, or even a nation newly carved from some older political system. In any case, it is an exciting venture, a challenging time of building something from nothing. It is the creative stage, the building stage, when all the energies of all the people are constantly poured into making the organization a bigger and better one.

The *second* stage is the time when growth is coming, progress is occurring, and the people of the institution divert time and energy from the building and creating function and devote it to organizing and managing what has been created. There is nothing particularly wrong with this. It is all necessary and important work. Offices must be decorated; staff must be hired; buildings must be built; policies must be elaborated; in short, the growing organization must be cared for. The problem is that this managerial work is usually done by the people who formerly were on the front end of the group, the building end. Now the work of creating new customers for the business—or new members for the church or new demand for the product—is done by staff members. It is subcontracted out, since the leadership of the group is very busy managing what has already been developed.

Stage *three* is the time when the primary concern becomes defending the acquisitions of the group from outside competition or encroachment. One business begins knocking its competitors, or seeking advantages against them. The organization becomes obsessed with safety, with hanging on to what it has, with little thought of making more of it. In the church, the energies are spent in "feeding the flock," serving the present members, working to keep the young people in the church. There is little time spent on making new converts.

The *fourth* stage is the point at which the energies of the group are turned inward, with members fighting among themselves to divide the spoils. By this time they have forgotten what it was like to be out there on the cutting edge, scraping to create and build from nothing. They assume that the "goodies" will always be there, that the money will always keep rolling in, and everyone fights for a bigger slice of the pie! There is arguing, squabbling, petty fusses, everyone working to justify his own importance, trying to get ahead of the next guy within the group. So the group stagnates. There is no atmosphere of excitement and mission. Nobody is making a new product, or bringing in new people. Growth stops. And as the pie shrinks, there is less for everyone, and so the fight becomes more rancorous. The downward momentum accelerates.

What is the answer to this downward spiral? *Go back to stage one!* When a group gets its eyes back on the original purpose of the organization, turns its attention back to creating new business or bringing in new people, the spiral can be reversed. The pastor gets out of his study and starts working directly to win new people; the officers of the company lay down their organizational charts to pour their energies into the sales effort of the business; things begin to happen! The growth graphs turn upwards again! When you go back to stage one, good things always begin to happen!

I guess that is why I like the Apostle Paul so much: he never got out of stage one! He never forgot what his job was, what the top priority was. He was a tiger! Once he got on the track, he never was distracted or slowed down. He was a mover, an action guy. He was thrown in jail, so he preached the Gospel to the jailer (*see* Acts 16). He was nearly drowned in a shipwreck and hit the beach preaching the Gospel (*see* Acts 27). He sat in a cell facing the chopping block and wrote letters talking about Jesus (*see* 2 Timothy). He had one speed—full steam; one direction—straight ahead; and only one priority—stage one!

What could happen would be fantastic if the church could get back to that kind of single-mindedness about its role in the world. If we could turn back to that basic goal of bringing new people into the Kingdom and into the church, all the other things —raising the budget, educating the people, helping the poor—would flow naturally from the enormous surge of vitality that would be triggered by all those new, excited Christians in the church. It never fails. When a congregation has become side-tracked by all the nitty-gritty routines of playing church, nothing jolts it back into the mainstream of evangelistic action like influx of new, enthusiastic Christians who have come into the Kingdom too recently to be jaded and ho-hum. The excitement of new converts inspires and motivates the old ones, and forces them to reassess their own commitment. The sleepy Christians are jolted into getting on with the Lord's work, and the momentum builds. But to start the ball rolling, there must be that flood of new believers, and that comes only when the church presses forward with its job of spreading the Gospel to those who do not yet know Jesus Christ as their personal Saviour.

Lord, make me a stage-one man!

9

Helen DeVos sits on the couch inside the motor home, a kind of rolling living room carrying its passengers across the Michigan countryside. She stabs intently at the piece of needlepoint in her lap and answers the question:

"What do I think about zero population growth? Well, I think stopping after two children is fine for those who want to do it. But I have four children and feel that is just about right for me.

"I realize what you are saying is true, that the world is facing terrible problems in the next generation. But that's all the more rea-

son to have children and bring them up
knowing how to help people. I have faith
that my children are going to help solve the
problems, rather than add to them."

Rich DeVos is being interviewed on one
of those daytime television shows on a local
station.

Interviewer: "You have a reputation for
being quite a family man, Mr. DeVos. I understand that you are quite a father. Is that
right?"

DeVos: "You'll have to ask my children
about that."

Two answers to two different questions,
separated by several months and many
miles, both suggesting much about the attitude of Mr. and Mrs. Richard DeVos toward
their family life. In one answer there is the
quiet confidence of a mother, the willingness to believe in the ultimate product of
her home, the unquenchable optimism that
even as unpredictable a thing as child rearing will turn out all right. In the other, there
is a gentle disclaimer, a candid reminder
that the important judgments of the quality
of one's parenthood rest most importantly
with the children themselves.

There are indications that family lies close to their hearts: a trip to the state capitol to receive an award includes all the grandparents; their table at a banquet is filled with nieces and nephews and relatives of every description; overseas business trips always include one of the children, with no brothers or sisters along to siphon off any of the attention; Dick, at nineteen the oldest son, is already opting for a career at Amway; a philanthropic fund is administered by the four children by majority vote without adult manipulation; and many other bits and pieces, slices of life too personal to mention, which add up to a couple who are hopelessly and irreversibly in love with their family.

BELIEVE!

. . . in the Family

When we speak of the survival of the American way of life, the concept conjures up visions of legislative assemblies, military arsenals, and the pomp and circumstance of governmental ceremony. In fact, the vitality of our American system depends not so much on any of these as it depends on what occurs in the living rooms, dining rooms, dens, and backyards of millions of ordinary, modest, American homes.

It would be difficult to arrange a hierarchy of the institutions which are most vital to our way of life. But it is safe to say that at the head of such a list would come the family. All other institutions—school, economic system, government, even the church—have their basis in the strength of the home and the family. Some sociologists have suggested that the family as we have traditionally known it will be extinct by the end of this century, gone the way of the dinosaur and the dodo bird. I don't believe that. I believe the family is so fundamental to human life that it will never be replaced by any other system. Still, one must admit that an increasingly complex culture has placed great stress on the family, that it no longer occupies the place of sanctity that it once had in the minds of many people.

It is time in America for the family concept to be reaffirmed, time for us to be prodded back to our basic responsibilities as parents, time for us to believe in the family so strongly that we will be willing to make whatever rearrangements of priorities are necessary to make our own homes the incubators of the American dream.

My grandparents came to this country from Holland and settled in western Michigan. I have warm memories of family life going back to earliest childhood. We were close to one another. We struggled sometimes, but we struggled together, and there was always plenty of love that never even had to be expressed in so many words. It was there, and as a child I always could sense it. I came by my interest in salesmanship honestly; my grandfather was an old-fashioned "huckster." He went to the farmer's market every day in an old truck, bought vegetables, and sold them in the community. I was with him the first time I ever sold anything, selling extra onions that he had left over after traveling his regular route.

My dad was an electrician and sold electrical supplies, so the tradition of selling was firmly imbedded in my family life. Dad was a wonderful man. He was as honest as any man who ever lived, and he worked hard all his life. He was frustrated by the fact that he never owned his own business, and his advice to become an independent businessman was one of the important motivating influences on me as a young man. He lived to see me achieve a certain degree of success; Amway had just started rolling when he died in 1962. I believe that before Dad died he had a feeling that Amway would become the success that it has. He told me that the foundation of the company had been honesty and fairness in our dealings; that the people of the company had come to count on Amway and what it stood for, and that I should not let them down. I have never forgotten that.

The point of such reminiscence is the

impact of the home in shaping lives. I can
look back and see clearly how important
my family was to my development. My attitude toward selling as a profession began
on that vegetable truck. My attitude toward
God began as we bowed our heads around
the dinner table. My belief in the power of
the will began as I ran along at my father's
heels and heard him talk of the limitless
potential of the human effort. The large
institutions of our society are made up of
people, and those people are more the product of the home than of any other single
influence. When I trace my own development in the home, and realize that as the
father of four children I am now on the
other side of the fence, I am sobered and
sometimes a bit frightened by the enormity
of the responsibility.

That responsibility is a joint one, with
the burden falling equally on the father and
the mother. But if one of the two fails to
take the responsibility seriously, the father
is more often than not the culprit. A man,
given the task of putting bread on the table,
seems to drift away from the demands of
the home more easily than the woman.

There is an old adage that says, "If you're
too busy to spend time with your family,

you're too busy." I believe that. There are
some tasks that cannot be delegated and
parenthood is one of them. There is no substitute for time spent in the home—quality
time, when the members of the family are
genuinely accessible to one another. At Amway we work hard to get our men home on
weekends. Our conventions never overlap
a Sunday. We are sometimes asked, "How
can you let your feelings about family life
keep you from making that extra profit?"
That is no problem with us. We have a simple philosophy: if the money must be made
at the expense of the family, we don't need
it. It is just not worth it.

I am away from home a lot, but when I
am there, I try to let my time be open to the
children, to have the time to do the things
they want to do. One of the best fathers I
know is our chief pilot. He is gone frequently, but when he is home, he is *really*
at home. He doesn't sit up and watch television all night; he is accessible to his children. The demands of businesses and careers
often are blamed for wrecking homes when
the job is not the true cause of the problem.
Very few jobs require so much time and
energy that a man cannot do them well and
still have time for his family. It is not usu-

ally the business that wrecks the home; it is the constant Saturdays and Sundays on the golf course, the time spent at the bar on the way home each evening, the nights out with the boys, and a variety of similar routines. The demands of the job become an "out," an excuse to neglect a marriage that is already failing or a homelife that is unpleasant.

Just being present in the home is only the beginning. The decisions to be made, the fine lines to be drawn between proper and improper use of discipline, are difficult and endless. In our family, the style of discipline has changed considerably since the earlier days. We went through the whole child-rearing routine of trying to let the children make their own decisions and reach appropriate choices on their own. That sounds good in the child-rearing books, but in our home it didn't work out so well, and as a consequence my own style has become more authoritarian. Certain rules are set and they are inarguable. The children are told, "These are the rules, and you are going to live with them. You can either live with them happily or you can bellyache about them and make us all miserable. But you *are* going to obey them." The trick, of course, is to decide which matters are important enough to warrant that kind of authoritarian approach and which are not.

No family is going to have smooth sailing all the time. If there is going to be a fight in my house over family discipline—and sometimes that is unavoidable—I insist on picking the battleground on which it will be fought. There are many things which irritate me, things which I would prefer to see my children do differently, but some of them are not worth making an issue of. I don't believe that a few inches of hair over a boy's collar is worth a major family hassle. I consider the kind of clothes my children wear an inappropriate battlefield on which to fight the war of adolescent rebellion. If I have to put my foot down, I want to do it on something that is really worth it!

Amway has always placed great emphasis on the family as a unit. We do not recruit men alone or women alone to sell our products when we can recruit the entire family. From the very first, our business has been something that husbands and wives—and even children—could do together. Jay Van Andel and I didn't sit down and say in the beginning, "This is going to be a family business." It just worked out that way. We saw that both the husband and the wife must be convinced before either would do well, so we decided to try to recruit them together. Gradually the family concept evolved, and now it is an important part of the Amway tradition.

At Amway we believe in the family enough to attempt to make involvement in our business something which strengthens family ties rather than threatening them. When we bring our distributors to Grand Rapids for sales seminars, we always bring husband and wife together. We give trips and cruises as incentive prizes, and the *couple* is always invited.

Even our conventions are family-oriented. When we had one of our first big conventions, the hotel where we held it doubled up on bartenders. Big convention here, they figured, so we'll sell lots of booze this weekend. They expected the bars to be humming. But on the first day the bars stayed empty all day. They couldn't believe it. And so the second day they pulled the extra bartenders off duty and doubled up the waitresses in the coffee shop. Why? Because the Amway crowd wasn't a bunch of guys away from home alone with nothing better to do than to stand around in a bar. It was families doing things together, sharing with each other, and that made for a whole different convention atmosphere.

I don't know the answers to the many questions about child rearing; I'm not sure anyone does. I don't know why some kids seem to absorb the values of their parents more than other kids do; I'll leave that one for the psychologists to worry about. I don't have any advice for young parents about how to run a family; I'm no authority on that. I just do the best I can to be a good father from day to day, and—like everyone else—I'll have to wait a few years to see how things turn out.

But on one point I am willing to be more emphatic: without strong families in America none of the values which we love and live for will survive—or, for that matter, will be worth preserving. Strong families are not made without strong people who believe enough in the value of their parenthood that they are willing to arrange their entire lives, if necessary, around home and family.

FIND A BETTER JOB!
IMPROVE YOUR PRESENT ONE!
SECURE YOUR FINANCIAL FUTURE!

Get the guidance and the understanding you need in these top-selling books of advice, analysis and how-to-do-it expertise!

_____ 42678	$3.50	**CRISIS INVESTING** by Douglas R. Casey
_____ 43516	$3.50	**COMPLETE RESUME BOOK AND JOB-GETTERS GUIDE** by Dr. Juvenal Angel
_____ 45265	$2.95	**COMPLETE REAL ESTATE ADVISOR** by Daniel J. deBenedictis
_____ 45765	$3.50	**MANAGERIAL WOMAN** by Margaret Hennig and Anne Jardim
_____ 82895	$2.95	**SALESWOMAN:** A Guide to Career Success by Barbara A. Pletcher

USE THE COUPON BELOW TO ORDER